CONTENTS

'This should be compulsory reading for all those who believe that the LisbonTreaty "should not be allowed to rest there" even after it has been ratified'
The Lord Tebbit CH

'I hope ministers, including Treasury ministers, will read this book'
Austin Mitchell MP (said on the floor of the House of Commons during a Parliamentary debate)

'... tells of this woman's nightmare at the hands of the EU'
Fr Brian McKevitt

'A gripping read'
Andrew Hamilton

'The full story'
Avril King

'This book exposes who the masters of corruption are ... An excellent exposé of the corrupt, undemocratic EU'
Matthew Davies

'So powerful I cannot stop thinking about it'
Frances Howard

'Her book reads like a chilling cross between two Kafka novels, *The Trial* and *The Castle* ... Shocking'
Christopher Booker

'A tour de force'
Emile Woolf

'You must read'
M Athanasiou

'The [EU] secrecy is outrageous. I want to cry'
A Crabtree

INTRODUCTION

WHY NOW?

This is the story of my experience at the European Union, a story that started in the Spring of 2001 and has not yet come to an end.

In these eight years I have come across people of different nationalities and cultural backgrounds, many of whom showed astonishment and at the same time admiration for my courage. Some would consider me a martyr, some a heroine, and there were also those who appeared so understanding that I guessed they had lived through a similar experience.

But I did not set out to become a martyr or a heroine, nor did I seek to become a public figure. It is because of the legal constraints of my case for wrongful dismissal, and thanks to my somewhat reserved personality, that it has taken me such a long time to write this book.

I have often been asked about the principles which guided me to adopt such a "courageous" attitude. I believe it can only be the result of the education received from my family and school: down to earth, common sense, realistic and non-selfish.

In all honesty I hate to be called a martyr, a heroine or even a courageous woman, as from my point of view, I was "simply doing my job". I was hired to reform a deficient accounting and financial management system and that is what I was trying to do. Under the EU treaties I was legally responsible for all the cash and assets of the EU. To fulfil that responsibility, I looked for support from the EU's political masters, but I did not get it.

When I joined the European Union I had almost 25 years of professional experience in financial management, mostly in the private sector, and a proven record of having done the right thing even in extremely difficult business situations. Should I give my reputation up for a well paid, theoretically powerful and life long job, with a generous pension at the end of it? It was a difficult decision.

I had many sleepless nights. I had to consider not only my own future life but that of my family, who had supported me all along. One night my husband gave me the crucial answer: "However much you try to ignore your nature you will never be able to sleep in peace if you bend to their demands." He was right. I had to respect my nature, and go wherever it led me.

Apart from the pressure to sign, and so authorize accounts and payments which I couldn't trust at all, what amazed me most was the arrogance which reigned in the institutions of the EU. There was no effort to show there was any commitment to transparency and accountability; no effort to show they might allow me the independence to decide what was the best way to reform the accounting system.

The other aspect that amazed me was how much all these bureaucrats had departed from the real world. It did not occur to them that somebody would challenge their long sustained arguments; it did not fit into their minds that a professional accountant would make her own evaluation without adhering to the state of denial in which they wished to live. They simply could not believe that anybody would be prepared to risk their job – that of European

Commission Chief Accountant, with the highest level of responsibility for EU funds – their pension and their professional career for the sake of defending integrity and getting the truth into the open.

No other civil servant in the EU has ever been treated in the way I was, with such disregard for human rights and cynical willingness to silence the truth. Not even those who were proved to have committed very serious offences were treated in such a harsh and denigrating manner.

Indeed, possibly no other case than mine has shown better how easily a bureaucracy – without any kind of external constitutional mechanism to correct or qualify its procedures – can become a tyranny.

And, crucially, the European Union's accounting systems remain in as lamentable state as ever – absorbing many billions of pounds of our money.

Yet this is the body in which European politicians appear determined to invest even more power, as the heart of a unified political entity.

I have written this book for those who cherish freedom, honest government and the true interests of the nations and peoples of Europe.

Marta Andreasen, MEP
July 2009

Note: A name marked with an asterisk at its first mention is not the real name.

How the EU Works

THE COMMISSION (unelected) has the monopoly of proposing all EU legislation, which it does in secret. Can also issue "Regulations", which are automatically binding in all Member States. It is run by a College of 27 COMMISSIONERS, currently one for each Member State, who are appointed for 5 years at a time. It has 37 branches, or "Directorates General", each run by a Director General. The "DGs" are the real bosses, and can rule for many years.

COREPER. The "Committee of Permanent Representatives", or bureaucrats who represent the Member States. A shadowy body, where the national horse-trading on the Commission's legislative proposals takes place, still in secret. The agreed versions of their proposals go to the Council of Ministers and the European Parliament for approval.

THE COUNCIL OF MINISTERS from Member States passes EU legislation, often by majority voting, and again in secret. The UK has 8.4% of the votes. Sometimes has to consult the European Parliament. Has the final say on Commission proposals, and could have supported Miss Andreasen.

THE EUROPEAN PARLIAMENT consists of 785 MEPs, elected every 5 years. The UK has 78. The Parliament cannot propose legislation but it can delay and even block it. In practice the MEPs do not want to de-rail their famous gravy train, so the 'project' proceeds. Can override the Commission on employment matters, and also could have supported Miss

Andreasen. (There are informal agreements which say that one EU institution should not interfere in the internal affairs of another.)

THE COMMISSION (again) becomes the sole enforcer of all EU legislation and decisions, supported when necessary by:

THE EUROPEAN COURT OF JUSTICE IN LUXEMBOURG (ECJ or LCJ). This is not an independent court of law; it is the engine of the "ever closer union of the peoples of Europe" required by the EU Treaties. It is financed by the EU, and has the final say on all EU matters, including employment cases. There is no appeal against its verdicts.

THE EUROPEAN COURT OF FIRST INSTANCE, hears cases before they reach the Luxembourg Court of Justice (above).

THE COURT OF AUDITORS, which is also financed out of the EU budget, is supposed to guarantee the proper use of EU funds to taxpayers. It has been unable to do this for the last 14 years. There are no external auditors.

Lord Pearson of Rannoch
May 2009

FOREWORD

By Lord Pearson of Rannoch

*If you want to go on hoping that the EU can be
"reformed from within", don't read this book.*

To anyone used to the disciplines of running a company in
this country, the story which follows is very difficult to
believe. And yet it is true. Billions of pounds of our taxpayers'
money are being sent every year to the European
Commission in Brussels, where they are literally unaccounted
for. Double-entry bookkeeping and accrual accounting are
strangers in the land. The EU's internal auditors have refused
to sign off its accounts for the last 14 years. There is no
independent auditor.

Yet this is the same EU which presumes to tell us how to run
so much of our lives, including our financial services and
accounting practices. 72% of the cost of UK regulations in
the last 10 years has been imposed by Brussels, for a total of
£106.6 billion, or more than £10 billion per annum.[1] When
you add in our share of EU spending, higher food costs and
our hard cash, our membership may be costing us around 8%
of GDP or £120 billion per annum, with no discernible
benefit.[2] How has this come about?

To understand the answer, we have to remember the big idea
which gave birth to the EU. That big idea was that the nation
states had been responsible for the carnage of two World

---

[1] "Out of Control? Measuring a decade of EU regulations", by Openeurope.org.uk
[2] "The Great European Rip-off", by The Taxpayersalliance.com.

Wars, and for the long history of conflict in Europe. Those nation states, with their unreliable democracies, therefore had to be emasculated, and diluted into a new form of supranational government, run by technocrats.[3]

From this genesis comes the EU's claim to have brought peace to Europe since 1945, which was in fact secured by NATO, heavily reliant on American force. The EU also pretends that it is needed to preserve that peace in future, which is equally untrue. Anyone who dares to challenge this propaganda is quickly labelled a Little Englander, a dangerous nationalist, or a xenophobic warmonger. The truth must not disturb the well-paid dream.

That original idea also explains why the monopoly for proposing all EU legislation still lies with the unelected bureaucracy: the Commission. Its draft laws are negotiated in COREPER (the Committee of Permanent Representatives), or bureaucrats from the member states, and agreed in the Council of Ministers, mostly by majority voting. The UK Government has some 8 per cent of that vote, and must accept whatever is decided. It still has a veto in some areas of our national life, but does not want to appear "anti-Communautaire" and so does not dare to use it. The whole process takes place in secret, and now imposes a large majority of our national law. The Commission then becomes the sole enforcer of all EU law, supported when necessary by the Luxembourg Court, against which there is no appeal.

The point is, of course, that this system is not accountable to anyone except itself. The British people elect and dismiss their Members of Parliament every five years or so, but our Parliament has no influence on the process of EU law making, or on what Brussels does with our money. Westminster is powerless even to query the fraud and waste, let alone to stop it.

---

[3] "The Great Deception" by Christopher Booker and Richard North. Continuum Books.

Europhiles pretend that the European Scrutiny Committees in the Commons and Lords inject an element of democracy into all this. But those Committees have no power, can look at only a tiny fraction of EU laws, and their suggestions go unheeded in Brussels. The Government has indeed promised that it won't sign up to a proposed EU law if either Committee is still considering it, but has broken that promise 435 times in the last 6 years.[4] No laws passed in Brussels have ever been overturned by Parliament, because the Treaties make sure that they can't be; that's the big idea, after all.

In theory, the European Parliament can block EU legislation, refuse to sanction the budget, and even throw out the entire Commission. But in reality the MEPs are far too dependent on their gravy train to risk de-railing it. The more the EU controls, the better for them; national accountability is their enemy.

Of course our political class doesn't want us to see that it has brought us so low; it prefers not to talk about it. Our three main parties refuse to support an official cost-benefit analysis of our membership, glibly asserting that the benefits are so obvious that it would be a waste of time.[5] The Government even dares to claim that 3 million UK jobs would be lost if we left the EU. But if we threw off the shackles of Brussels regulations, and continued in free trade with our friends in Europe, jobs would in fact be created. And there really isn't any doubt that our free trade with the EU would indeed continue, because they sell us more than we sell them. We are their largest client.

Another killer point in the Eurosceptic locker is that only some 9% of our gross domestic product goes in trade with the EU, in deficit; around 11% goes to the rest of the world, in surplus, and some 80% stays right here in our domestic economy. But the dictats from Brussels hit the whole of our

[4] HM Government Written Answer, House of Lords, 15/1/09, Col. WA166.
[5] Debates in the House of Lords 27/6/03, 11/2/04 and 8/6/07.

economy, meaning that our healthy 91% dog is being wagged by its mangy 9% tail.[6]

For good measure the share of UK exports going to the EU is shrinking, while our exports to the rest of the world are growing.[7]

When pressed on these obvious disadvantages of our membership, our politicians say it is justified because being in the EU gives them greater influence on the world stage.[8] So the EU is remote, inevitable, boring.

Yet the EU is also a brilliant trap. It is illegal under the Treaties which we have signed to repatriate even the smallest power to this country without the unanimous agreement of all the other 26 member states. So any "reform from within" is so unrealistic as to be unobtainable, and is designed to be so. The only way out is the door.

And the controlling bureaucracy in Brussels numbers only a few tens of thousands of people. The trick is that their dictats have to be executed by the millions of civil servants in the member states, with no interference from elected Parliaments, or the people they represent.

Nothing illustrates better the corruption which such absolute power spawns than the story of Marta Andreasen.

Malcolm Pearson
House of Lords, July 2009

---

[6] See Globalbritain.org Briefing Note no 22.
[7] See Globalbritain.org Briefing Note no 52.
[8] Debates in the House of Lords on the Lisbon Treaty 2008.

CHAPTER I

RECRUITMENT

When I first read the ad it seemed like it could almost have been specially written for someone of my background, experience and aspirations. The European Commission was advertising for a Budget Execution Director. Born in Buenos Aires, in Argentina, and educated at an English school there, the daughter of a Danish father and with a mother of French origin, I had long been trilingual in Spanish, English and French, and I felt comfortable in Italian.

In the early summer of 2001, I was 46 and had studied accountancy and economics at universities in Argentina, Spain and the United States. I had worked for some 20 years for a variety of British and American multinationals, and more recently with the OECD in Paris. My husband, Octavio, also an economist, had to travel a great deal working in the private sector.

But between us we had organised it so that there was always one of us at home with the children, if the other was travelling. Martin, then 19, and 16-year-old Carolina had always amply reciprocated our love and worked hard at their studies. There was no question that we wouldn't keep our home in one of Europe's most handsome and vibrant cities: Barcelona. There were direct, two-hour flights to Brussels. So what were the problems?

"What do you think, Octavio?" I asked passing him the copy

of The Financial Times. Octavio pondered the advertisement for a while. "Interesting," he finally pronounced, "but possibly challenging."

Though we had met and married in Argentina, and been Spanish citizens for only 15 years, it was long enough to see the good side of the European Union. Massive EU subsidies had helped transform Spain's primitive infrastructure with new roads, bridges, rail links. Indeed, it was exhilarating to be part of Spain's maturing democracy, moving steadily forward from the dark days of Franco's heavy-handed, sclerotic rule.

My previous job, with the OECD, had not been easy. After joining in 1998, as head of accounting, I had noticed serious problems with its systems, and raised my concerns with management. When I had suggested reforms, they disagreed completely. Subsequently, they had hired Arthur Andersen to do an independent report which criticized the OECD's internal accounting systems as "outdated and inadequate," and confirmed the soundness of my proposals. But by that time I had been suspended from the job.

Not even that experience, however, had diminished my ambition to work – and, as I then hoped, even do some good – in the public sector.

So it was that I applied for the European Commission job and was delighted to be invited for an interview in mid-July, 2001, with Jean Maison*, Director General and thus the most senior civil servant in the Budget Directorate. Then 60, of small build, with dark brown eyes and sallow hue, he was neatly-dressed in a dark suit.

Somewhat formal, reserved, he seemed a typical 'Enarque' – a product of France's highly-selective Ecole Nationale d'Administration and a member of that formidable elite which has probably served its country's interests better than any other bureaucracy on earth.

Maison's deputy, Jens Mogen* a large, well-built, fair-haired Swede, was also present for part of that first interview. But Maison, who had already been in his current, virtually all-powerful post of Budget Director General for 13 years, clearly dominated his department.

I flew back to Barcelona with no great hopes. What was it? Somehow, I felt that I had not done myself credit. My CV, by any standards, had to seem interesting, impressive even - certainly in terms of the job they were trying to fill. Yet I had managed to find out little more about what that job entailed.

As Maison clearly struggled with English, we had switched to French half way through the interview. Had that been an irritation, a humiliation for him? How comfortable would he feel working with a woman in a senior position?

Somehow, I couldn't put my finger on what it was that was niggling me. Maybe it was simply that I had got absolutely no spark of warmth from him. He was correct – as one would expect of an enarque and Frenchman of his stratospheric level. But there was no real sense of him actually welcoming me as a future colleague.

Back home at our flat in Barcelona, Octavio was as warm and supportive as ever. He was philosophical. "It can't be the end of the world, Marta, if you don't get this job."

We were both aware of the recent turmoil within the European Commission, when two years earlier Commission President Jacques Santer and all his fellow Commissioners had had to resign following revelations by a Dutch EC official, Paul van Buitenen, of widespread wrongdoing.

The detail that thrilled news editors round Europe was the fact that Commissioner Edith Cresson, a former French Prime Minister no less, had given her live-in dentist a lucrative research contract on AIDS – a subject for which he had no qualifications. At the end of 18 months – and payment of some 136,000 euros – he had produced 24 pages of notes which were generally agreed to be of almost no scientific value.

But as an accountant, I knew that if senior figures felt free to casually disburse such largesse, there was clearly room to improve the Commission's accounting systems.

After the meltdown of the Jacques Santer Commission in 1999, there had been an independent committee of five "Wise Men" to examine how the Commission dealt with cronyism, fraud and mismanagement. They had suggested far-reaching reforms.

While scandals were still being exposed, I chose to believe that there had been a change of culture. Further, I rationalized that if they were recruiting a professional accountant from outside the Commission, with a brief to work on the reforms promised in response to the "Wise Men's" report, then they must be serious about radical change.

For these reasons, I still felt buoyant when invited for a second interview in Brussels on September 11, 2001. Straight off a flight from Barcelona, I was for some while out of touch with events unfolding 3,000 miles away across the Atlantic. For at about the time my interview should have been starting – at 3pm Brussels time – the World Trade Center was crumbling horrifically in New York.

For half an hour, secretaries and assistants fluttered round me on the 12th floor of the Breydel 1 building, as their bosses deliberated on whether they should evacuate the building. Maybe this gleaming glass and steel icon of European solidarity might also be seen as a legitimate target.

Wryly, I considered the shambolic security arrangements that I had just been through myself on the ground floor of the building. After announcing myself as coming for an interview with the Secretary General of the European Commission, I was just nodded through. My name was on no list. There was no ID check and, indeed, nothing to record visitors to the building. When I turned towards the security equipment for scanning bags and people, I was waved on. "Machine's not working," a guard commented nonchalantly.

Finally, at 3.30pm I was ushered into a vast interview room – and was immediately struck by the old-fashioned nature of the arrangements. For in the private sector jobs I had applied for, there might be many interviews – but never with more than one or two people at a time, and usually seated on a sofa and easy chairs.

On this occasion, rather like the defendant in some judicial process, I found myself seated alone on one side of a long oval table. Sitting opposite was the Commission Secretary General John Castle*, a well-groomed, 48-year-old Irishman, Budget Director General Jean Maison and some six others. Speaking in English, once again we went through my qualifications for the job and the experience I had had in handling large numbers of staff.

As we concluded, Castle graciously asked if I had any questions. I did. I asked for a fuller description of the job and the expectations for the incumbent.

Immediately, Maison, who had until then been silent, jerked forward and complained, in French, that I was turning round the whole sense of the interview

Clearly discomforted by this intervention, Castle smoothed things over as best he could. He told me that that sort of information would be given to those short-listed for the job.

I had another question. "What happened to the last person who was doing this job?" The answer – not terribly clear and which later turned out to be wholly untrue – was that he had been sick and had died.

Once again, I returned to Barcelona without any great expectations. Indeed, seven days later I received an e-mail from the Commission's Administration Directorate informing me that I had not been selected for the short-list. A week after that I was rung up by one of those who had interviewed me on September 11, to let me know that Commissioner Michaele Schreyer – head of the Budget Directorate and therefore Maison's political boss – wanted me to continue the recruitment process, despite the fact that I had not been short-listed by the Nomination Committee.

Surprised, and somewhat bemused, I agreed on the basis that further interviews took place in Barcelona. To this they agreed – apart from the final interview with Commissioner Schreyer herself.

This took place at the end of October, with just Schreyer, Maison and myself, in the Commissioner's office on the 15th floor of the Breydel 2 building. A massively wide panoramic view over the rooftops of Brussels offered some relief from the Commissioner's chosen decor of chairs in chrome and purple velvet, and an emerald green carpet.

Michaele Schreyer, then 51, had been a big figure in German Green politics and had served as a Minister of Urban Development and Environmental Protection in the state government of Berlin. Green-eyed and fair-haired, formal, intense, she came across to me as not terribly sure of herself, but a degree warmer than Maison.

As she had no French, and I had no German, she spoke in her uncertain English. With a degree in economics and sociology, she showed an intelligent interest in my experience in managing large teams, my acquaintance with accrual accounting and with a German financial software package which she said was being introduced.

As at the previous meeting, Maison said nothing until towards the end. "If offered the job, would you be prepared to accept a five-year contract as a temporary worker?" Somewhat taken aback, I could only respond, "I would have to think about that."

For three weeks I heard nothing more until rung at home in Barcelona by Schreyer who wanted to know what I felt about Maison's proposal of my working on a temporary basis. I told her of my reservations. "Surely, this will put me at a disadvantage in relation to the more than 130 people on my staff all of whom have jobs for life – particularly in view of there being a reform programme." I mentioned that I had had difficulties with this at the OECD and told her about what led to my suspension.

Schreyer sought to be reassuring and told me that at the European Commission I would not have to go through the same situation as at the OECD and that the management would be supporting me a hundred per cent in all my efforts. She added that I would certainly be given plenty of time to get well acquainted with the job.

Following her call there was one from Maison who expressed surprise that Schreyer had not yet made me a specific offer. Bluntly, he informed me that I was her choice – but certainly not his. He went on to offer me a three-year contract, with one additional year on automatic renewal.

Politely, I pointed out, "But this is even less than what was mentioned at our last meeting." I told him that I would think about it and get back to him as soon as possible.

Before I had had a chance to do so there was an e-mail from one of Maison's staff. This pointed out that the Administration Directorate had informed them that the contract could only be for two years – plus the one for automatic renewal. At that point, I rang Schreyer to tell her that under these conditions I could not accept the offer. She was not in her office and so I left my message with her cabinet assistant.

And that I thought was that.

Three weeks later – it was now early December 2001 – I received an e-mail grandly informing me that the European Commission had approved my nomination as Accounting Officer and Budget Execution Director as a permanent official. This was the first time that the Commission had mentioned my recruitment using two different titles. They went on to inform me that, in the course of discussions on my appointment, they had discovered that the Accounting Officer of the European Commission could not be a temporary employee. Brilliant!

There was also the formality of my having to pass a medical examination – which had to be done in Brussels – and had to be done quickly as they now wanted me in post by January 1, 2002. So after five months of prevarication, confusion and delay, it was now all systems go.

Mystery deepened when, before I had even received the letter confirming the details of my appointment, I got an e-mail from one Charles Cash*, head of the Treasury Unit – one of the five unit heads who would be reporting to me in my new post in the Budget Directorate. Would he be able to see me when I came to Brussels for my medical? He knew the date.

Somewhat premature – and barely appropriate – I knew that such a meeting would really not be convenient. I was making only a flying visit to Brussels for the medical. I was in the midst of organising a family Christmas in Barcelona and had about a thousand other things to do before starting a new job.

Yet I didn't want to appear inflexible or unfriendly. Somewhat reluctantly, I agreed to meet at my hotel the night before the medical. With the flight delayed by an hour, it was already 11pm when I finally got to my hotel on the icy night of December 15.

In the almost deserted hotel lobby, a figure in immaculate dark blue coat, and with Homburg hat, rose to greet me with the most gracious of smiles. A 62-year-old Briton, with thinning white hair and of impeccable dress, Charles Cash set off on a rambling explanation of the security arrangements being made in the 'European quarter' of Brussels for the forthcoming Laeken council. This was being held to make the EU ".. more democratic, transparent and efficient." Wonderful.

So why did we have to go into all of this at that time of night? I was bone tired. I just wanted to go to bed. But then fumbling in his pockets for some document to do with my recruitment, Cash suddenly switched the subject and referred to the Budget Director General as a not at all easy man to work with. Bright, very bright, but he could treat people quite harshly. Cash was afraid I might find him rather discouraging about any changes I might have in mind.

Speechless for a moment, I was now doubly on my guard. Warily, I restricted myself to murmuring generalities about my hopes ".. of having a good relationship with everyone, particularly with the staff on whom I know I will have to rely."

In bed, I pondered the oddity of the meeting. Could this man actually be an emissary from Maison himself – in a last desperate effort to make me turn down the job?

CHAPTER II

MY FIRST MONTH IN OFFICE

On January 3, 2002, still full of enthusiasm, I arrived to find Euro-Brussels almost deserted. As instructed, I went to the Administration Directorate to find that they had absolutely no record of my recruitment. With my name not on their database, they were unable to register me or even issue me with a badge. "Your file should have been completed by the office of the Budget Director General." (Maison again.)

"Why not call the Personnel Directorate?" I suggested. "They were the people who issued the letter confirming my employment." But that did nothing to sort out the problem. They said the Budget Directorate should have completed my file so that they could process my recruitment. But they had failed to do this before my arrival and most of their staff were now on holiday.

Finally, I made my way to the Budget Directorate building – Breydel 2 – to ask Charles Cash, my late-night visitor of two weeks earlier, if he could get me into the building. And so, for my first two weeks, I had to go in as a 'visitor.'

At least I had an office – and one with a fine view – on the eighth floor of the building, with an outer office with desks for two secretaries. The shelves in my office were already stocked with a complete set of EU Treaties and accompanying volumes of regulations. I had plenty to read.

Cash and the other senior staff I met seemed keen to impress upon me the lack of resources and the small amount of attention devoted by the Commission to the accounting and treasury management of the EU budget. Some of this I dismissed as the usual grumbles of almost every organization I had worked in – but I could see that there were some issues that had started long before my arrival.

Maison himself, in fact, did not appear until my second week. Every Monday, he held a meeting in his 13th floor office with the four Directors in his Budget Directorate and it was there that I met my three Director colleagues, of equivalent grade 2 rank. Maison graciously welcomed me and then moved briskly on to the first item for discussion: the role of the Commission's Internal Audit Directorate, which had been created after the debacle of the Jacques Santer Commission.

The post of Director General, in this new Directorate, was held by a Dutchman, Jules Muis. Although I was still picking up on the coded language of the Commission, and said little myself during that meeting, I quickly sensed some sort of turf war warming up.

There was some prim talk about what ".. the role of the new post of Director General of Internal Audit should or should not be .." from which I deduced that Maison did not welcome Muis poking his nose too closely into the affairs of the Budget Directorate.

During this, my second week in office, I met more of my five heads of unit, and others on my staff, both individually and in groups. I also heard more on the lack of appreciation from the hierarchy on their work and financial responsibility.

Still in that hectic second week, Pierre Sachet*, a Director of the Luxembourg-based Court of Auditors, had asked to come and meet me, together with a colleague. As this was still only my seventh working day in office, I felt that it was far too early for such a meeting – but I was then given to understand that the meeting was to be something in the nature of a courtesy visit.

Some courtesy visit! No sooner had they sat down in my office than Sachet launched into the attack. Sternly, he announced that they were expecting a lot from me. During the many years they had been criticizing the accounting, Maison had ignored all their requests for reform and all they had received were promises of change. What they now wanted from me was *action*.

His colleague, head of unit Wilfred Van Dyck*, next pitched in with a blistering diatribe about the accounting, the management of the budget, the lack of professional knowledge. By that time the Court of Auditors had, for the previous six years, refused to approve the EU's annual accounts, so one could see they had a point. Nevertheless, I was still startled at such a complete lack of discretion with someone who had only just joined the organization. Maybe at least I would have some valuable allies in any future battles.

But two weeks later I heard that, with a reorganization of the Court of Auditors, those two officials would not be responsible for the EU accounts much longer. So why the rush to see me?

At Maison's next Directors' meeting, he referred to the 'draft assurance report' from the Court of Auditors for the year 2000, and asked if I, as Commission Chief Accountant, could go along to the Budget Committee of the Council of Ministers that same day. Again, I was staggered that I was being invited – barely two weeks into the job, and with so little warning – to explain any deficiencies in the accounts for an entire year when I was not in office. I was still trying to find these out for myself.

The experience – with some 25 of us seated round a large rectangular table in the Council's Justus Lipsus building, was nevertheless enlightening. The Budget Committee started by extending to me their sincere wishes of success in a "terribly difficult" job. These pleasantries out of the way, head of unit Wilfred Van Dyck and other representatives from the Court of Auditors, spoke at length about the deficiencies of the accounts for 2000.

But the reaction of the Council's committee – made up of political representatives from the governments of the member states – was uniformly mild, verging on the narcoleptic. I left the meeting with two key questions in my mind. Why were the people there, who ought to know, so keen to stress that my job was "terribly difficult?"

More important, why did those in the upper echelons of the EU – both civil servants in the Commission and politicians in the Council of Ministers – appear to be in such denial about the magnitude of the EU's problems? Did they live in some sort of bubble? Didn't they read the papers? Were they simply not aware of the scandals being reported almost daily in the European press?

One of the murkiest scandals had originated in my own country of Spain, in the cultivation of high-grade flax. With subsidies worth five times the support available for cereals, farmers had responded by raising flax cultivation from 186 hectares to 91,000 hectares – an increase of nearly 50,000 per cent – in five years. No matter that the flax was of such low-grade that it had no conceivable market.

According to a report by Spain's anti-fraud office, much of the crop for which grants were claimed was in any case fictitious. Processing plants simply issued false certificates to draw in extra subsidies. As Spanish investigators closed in on what was happening, much of the evidence and crop went up in smoke. Over the course of a month, there were seven separate fires at linen producers' premises.

Some of the scheme's beneficiaries – costing EU taxpayers up to 75 million euros a year – were said to be working in the office of the Spanish agriculture minister in the late 1990's: Miss Loyola de Palacio. Well illustrating the prevailing EU culture, one Spanish government spokesman, widely quoted in the European press, sought to explain, "Don't blame Loyola de Palacio – blame the Common Agricultural Policy. The EU gives lots of subsidies for things that are never consumed, and even for things that aren't planted. She was just looking after the interests of the farmers, which was her job."

Two of her ministerial appointees did eventually resign. Miss Loyola de Palacio, apparently unaware of flax profiteering by her staff, had later moved on to her then current Brussels post, controlling one of the EU's largest budgets, as Commissioner for transport and energy. (Later still, she was to become a Vice President of the Commission.)

Yet the more I probed into the affairs of my own department, the more I could see how the lack of controls made such scandals possible. There was little separation of duties – so that directors running programmes were also often authorising payments. Indeed, when I began going through reports and acquainting myself with the computer procedures, I could scarcely believe the haphazard way in which much of the accounting was done.

Numbers in the computerized reports often changed from day to day. Some of the accounts came in on spreadsheets on which anyone could make changes – and thus, if these were manipulated, leave no electronic trail. Some of the accounting did not even incorporate double-entry book-keeping – a system invented by the Italians in the 16th century – in which the two effects of every financial transaction are recorded: first, where the money comes from or goes to and, secondly, what is the item or service that is being paid for or received.

The computer systems were a mess – with sub-systems that were not entirely compatible, so that some information was lost or corrupted within the interface. Clearly, the people who had designed or modified the system knew little about advanced computer system capabilities, and even less about accounting.

Scarily, thousands of payments were being made out of the budget every week – for serious sums of money – and I was the one who would ultimately bear responsibility for them. So, for a start, I asked for a list of all those who could – electronically – authorize such payments. But this was not forthcoming – ever.

One of the first things I found out was that the opening balance for the EU accounts for 2001 didn't match the closing balance for the 2000 accounts. There was a gap of almost 200 million euros. These accounts were actually published in the official journal of the European Union, as all EU accounts had been and still are. Had no one noticed?

When I asked my staff to explain the discrepancy, I was informed that these were loans given to third parties and then written off. Watching my manners and blood pressure as best I could, I strove to explain that if this had really been the case the sums should have been written off in the prior year or the new year as non-recoverable. "You can't just have these sums disappearing between the two years. All this money was provided by European taxpayers."

The contempt with which this money was being treated caused me real alarm. "How could you just write this money off?" I asked. "Who would have authorized it?" But I never got answers to such questions. And indeed, it was not just one specific case that concerned me, but the whole notion that the system could operate in this way: that money, not approved in the budget, could be advanced to anyone, be called a loan and then be written off when the recipient failed to return it.

Over the next month, I spoke to some of my staff who were

not willing to admit to shortcomings in the system. Others, however, were clearly embarrassed by the unprofessional way in which many of the transactions were carried out and the almost arbitrary manner in which financial information was passed on from the Commission's various Directorates.

Soon, I came up against particular problems in the "recoveries" section – one of the five units that reported to me. As most of the EU budget is paid out in advance – that is before the specific programme which has been proposed in the budget is actually run – there was clearly ample opportunity for loss of control.

In most private companies, the recovery section would claim back money when there was no documentary evidence that goods or services had been received. Similarly, in organizations like the EU, which pay out subsidies, this section would be in charge of recovering funds where there was no proper documentation to confirm that the subsidy had been used for its approved purpose. But I was amazed to discover that in the Commission there was NO central register of the recipients of all funds paid out – so the recovery process was doomed to failure from the start.

In the absence of a central register, the information on necessary repayments was provided by the Directors General of the different Commission Directorates, who in turn had to rely on those who had actually been given the money. This is like a bank relying on its debtors to tell it how much money it is owed!

The only record kept centrally by the Accounting Services referred to what was known as "direct payments" – that ten per cent of the budget paid directly to the supplier of a service or goods, which created so much of the controversy over fraud and irregularities in the EU accounts.

Incredibly, nobody appeared to be worried about the control of the other 90 per cent of "indirect payments" – where the Commission paid funds to a local agency or ministry in one of the member states, who then passed on the money to the final beneficiary.

I was staggered that the issue had been treated with such neglect over the years. The Commission hierarchy could not be ignorant of this failure when every year the Court of Auditors repeated their same damning criticism of EU accounting. Yet every year the stock response was that any gaps in the accounts would be replenished by the recovery of overpaid funds – when in fact such recovery simply wasn't feasible.

In the meantime, and as from my second week in office, documents for my signature began piling up on the meeting table in my office. These documents prompted me to ask for more information before I felt able to sign. Most of this further information either took a long time to come, or was never supplied.

At a time when I should have been sorting out these and so many other basic issues, I became involuntarily involved in moving the accounting being done by ISPRA – a Commission research centre in Italy – to Brussels. This was a move that had been decided on by Maison long before my arrival and, technically speaking, could well have been handled by others.

But Maison was insistent – and Charles Cash was also exerting ostensibly helpful efforts on this issue. Cash, in fact, had already scheduled a meeting for us both to fly down to Varese, in Italy, on January 17, the third week after my recruitment.

On the flight down, Cash assured me that Maison had been there to tell staff that the accounting section would be closed and that new jobs would be found for those not wanting or able to move to Brussels. Only hazily briefed, I was under the impression that I would just be part of a discussion that involved some dozen senior staff.

In the event, neither their direct unit head, nor their

Director General attended the meeting. Just before it started, Cash evaporated, making noises about some ".. urgent telephone call."

So it was I – a Commission official for little more than two weeks – who had to broach painful issues. As soon as I opened my mouth I realized that I was speaking to people who couldn't believe what they were hearing. "But Monsieur Maison came here two months ago to tell us that there would be no closure for at least two years and that everything would stay the same," volunteered one. Another stood up to point out, "We were specifically told that any rumors we might hear about this were wrong."

In short, as far as I could establish, nothing had been done to find these employees new jobs – and yet, as the inadvertent bearer of bad news, my name was the one that would be mud in that corner of the Commission!

On behalf of these ISPRA employees, I felt appalled. It stirred uncomfortable memories of some of the allegations that had been made before the 1999 collapse of the Santer Commission. Before that, there had been the pungent comments of the British economist Bernard Connolly, a Commission official fired after writing his book, The Rotten Heart of Europe: The Dirty War for Europe's Money. This targeted what he saw as the Commission's "distortion and manipulation" of the facts of the EU moving towards a single monetary union.

"The more blatantly obvious the falsehood, the more insistently its perpetrators repeat it. My decision to write this book ... was born first of incredulity at the hundreds of 'black is white' statements made about the ERM (Exchange Rate Mechanism), and then of anger at the treatment given to anyone who tried to point out the lies."

But could things still really be that bad?

When later I mentioned to Maison the misunderstanding I had had to deal with at ISPRA, the Director General simply looked at me, as if bemused that there could have been a problem. Clearly, the labour directives that had been pouring out of Brussels, instructing employers all round Europe on how they should treat – and consult with – their staff, didn't carry too much weight within the Commission itself.

The day after my bruising meeting at ISPRA there was another scarcely happier meeting in Brussels. Maison had called a meeting at which various matters were to be discussed. One of them concerned ".. the annual programme of work .." for my department.

This was in fact the first time that I had heard of this or been shown any documentation. There, I saw it written down that it was expected that the "accounting reform communication" would be completed "within three months of the incorporation of the new Accounting Officer."

Having seen what I already had of the then current system, and knowing my need to find out a lot more, I had to tell Maison, "I can't possibly commit to that date." Maison was not happy. His anger simply increased when he asked who I had in mind as project leader for the changes, and I told him, "I believe that I should be project leader. Given my experience of such reforms, I believe that they will need both a project leader and a project manager."

Then Maison told me whom he had in mind as project leader: Mara Villos*. She was a woman who reported to me, and at that time was simply acting as head of the general accounting unit in the absence of a sick colleague.

It was obvious that if she continued doing her current job, she could not also act as effective project leader. It was like a company building a new factory, which still needed a competent leader to keep the old one running.

But as Mara Villos was also present at that meeting, there was clearly a limit as to how far that discussion could be pursued.

As the meeting broke up, Maison's assistant, Theodor Lemercier* approached to counsel me, "You must not go against the Director General on his decision of project leader. He has a very high opinion of Mara Villos and of the work she has done." I explained that as Commission Accounting Officer, it was only natural that I should lead the reform. But clearly, I was having difficulty in picking up on the attitudes that seemed to characterize so much of the Commission proceedings.

Needless to say that meeting, like so many others, left me with a mass of unanswered questions. Why was Maison getting involved in an accounting reform for which I was responsible as Chief Accountant? Why did he have to decide who would lead the reform? If he was so convinced that his choice was up to the job, why had they not started the reforms two years earlier – rather than waiting for my arrival?

In a meeting with my staff a couple of days later we discussed a draft commentary, prepared in June 2001, on the "modernization of the accounting system." This had never become final – nor had any of the actions listed in it, by then long overdue, ever been brought into operation.

But what was even more worrying was that the document didn't even begin to deal with the really radical changes needed to the entire computer system – and for whose unreliability I had already seen ample evidence.

At the next Directors' meeting with Maison, I felt it time for me to start reporting on my serious concerns. I spoke at some length of the growing list of questions I had asked on authorizations and payments that had not been answered. I talked of my concern at the apparent incompatibility of two of the sub-systems of the computer system that processed financial transactions.

When I finished, no one uttered a word and Maison simply moved on to another subject: the future of the EU budget and a new Financial Regulation (EU accounting law) on which I would have to respond before the Budget Committee in the Council of Ministers.

This proposed eliminating the existing "Validity of discharge for payment." In a word, this meant that payments could be processed directly to the bank by different Directorates – without my staff checking the supporting documents to establish that the payment was for the right amount, for the approved purpose and was going to the right person.

I couldn't believe that an institution like the Commission would want to operate in such a lax way, particularly after the Santer Commission had had to resign over allegations of financial mismanagement. When I shared my alarm with some of my staff, one of them related, with a knowing smile, that when he had mentioned this 'reform' to a friend working for a big private corporation, his friend had suggested that it looked as if the change had been deliberately designed to *eliminate* controls.

But, I still wanted to believe that such a proposal was the result of ignorance.

On January 22, I was able to share just a few of my concerns with Jules Muis, first Director General of the newly-created Internal Audit Directorate. He had rung my secretary to suggest a meeting. A tall, white-haired, blue-eyed, fresh-faced, affable Dutchman, then aged 57, he was a very different animal from any I had yet met at the Commission. He had had a sparkling career in various private corporations, but also well knew the ways of the public sector. Head-hunted to sort out a mess at the World Bank, he had served there for six years, as Vice President and Controller.

Although I was naturally guarded in my response to questions on how I was getting on with Maison, I spoke of my main concerns about the computer system and the changes proposed in the new Financial Regulation. He already clearly appreciated the enormity of problems facing the Commission.

He referred to an audit he had made on the accounting system which revealed serious shortcomings. He had asked Budget Commissioner Michaele Schreyer to address them and allow him to make a full audit – but had so far met with massive resistance. This all fitted in with the comments I had heard from Maison about Muis at my first Directors' meeting.

Despite the problems he himself faced, Muis still appeared to enjoy life, and could joke about Commission staff being adept " at steering you into trees and keeping you busy with the unimportant things, while the big things are going on behind the scenes." Recalling my own calamitous trip to ISPRA in Italy, I already well knew what he meant. "If you need any help in what you are doing," Muis concluded, "don't hesitate to come and ask."

As money daily poured out of the Commission coffers, I was amazed at being given signatory authority before I had received a document formalizing my recruitment as a civil servant. Indeed, it wasn't until some four weeks after my arrival that I was to receive this formal authority – known as the "nomination act."

In the event, I was eventually presented with two such documents. One related to my role as Chief Accounting Officer, the other as Budget Execution Director. Both were signed by Romano Prodi, then President of the European Commission. But whereas the first came to me directly from Prodi's office, the other came from Maison's office – to be signed for by myself – a formality I later realized intended to make it clear that I came within Maison's authority as Budget Execution Director. But would this restrict my independence?

While the EU Treaties are clear about the Chief Accountant reporting to the College of Commissioners, there was always an obscurity about my role as Budget Execution Director that I never fully penetrated. Indeed, I was never given a clear, full job description for either of the two jobs.

Lack of clarity bedevilled much of the work of the Commission, and I soon found myself dragged into endless internal squabbles. One concerned fellow Director Jacques Mon* – who was head of the Directorate's central services, responsible, among other things, for ensuring the good functioning of the computer systems on which financial transactions were processed. He wrote me a letter asking me to sort out the 'reconciliation' of figures – ensuring the consistency and compatibility of data coming from different sources – that were being fed into two of the computer's sub-systems.

Circulating this request among my staff, I was promptly told that they had just lost – to Mon's team – the very people doing the work that they were now being asked to do. I could only back them up on that point.

Next, I was involved in a crisis meeting with the staff in charge of Recoveries. They were responsible not only for recovering overpaid funds but for collecting fines imposed by the Commission. They wanted to discuss the case of a company unable to pay a fine because of financial problems.

As Chief Accountant, I was the only one able to grant extended payment terms – provided the company could produce a bank guarantee. The meeting with the company's representatives took place two hours later – and was also attended by staff from the Competition Directorate who had imposed the fine. They appeared happy to accept the explanation they had been given of the company's financial difficulties. I was not.

In fact, I was puzzled as to how they felt qualified to comment on the fined company's financial affairs – and why they had brought me to this meeting if they were making such judgments for themselves.

I asked to see the financial statements – and noticed that the company was part of a group. I asked for the group statements and found them almost identical – apart from the name of the company being changed for that of the group. The Competition staff seemed to me to be happy to overlook this 'detail' – and eager to bounce me into accepting the financial paperwork as sufficient guarantee. I refused to do so.

The following day I was invited to attend a working group on fines, chaired by the deputy Director General of the Competition Directorate. He outlined the problem they had when wanting to impose a fine on a company claiming insolvency. In a further meeting, his staff drew attention to the amount of time involved in analysing the financial statements of fined companies.

"But that is not your job," I pointed out. "That is the job of the accounting services – both because of the knowledge required and also to avoid a conflict of interest." I went on to stress that they should know better than me, given their time with the Commission, that the rules were quite clear on not granting any extended terms unless a bank guarantee was provided.

"Do you understand that there could be a conflict of interest in your intervening in the negotiation of the payment of a fine?" I asked. Heads were duly nodded as they agreed that they did. Yet this was certainly not the last time I was hauled in to face a stark choice: either agree to payment terms that were clearly unacceptable under EC rules – or risk appearing an ogre in front of third parties.

At the last Directors' meeting of that first month, discussion turned to the Annual Declaration that the Directors General would have to sign, for the first time, for the 2001 accounts. I spoke again of my concern about the lack of compatibility between the two sub-systems in which the transactions were processed and the fact that the system did not cover all financial transactions. The fundamental problem with the

Directors General signing the Annual Declarations is that the figures they have in their Directorates' systems do not add up to the total of the EU accounts.

I said, "This means that the Accounting Services, that's us, have to send each Director General another set of accounts that do add up. The Directors General then refuse to take responsibility for what they consider 'unreliable' accounts which do not correspond with the figures they have been putting into the system."

Maison then had a brainwave. Why doesn't the Chief Accountant send the accounts to the various Directorates – signed by him/her assuming responsibility for their reliability and accuracy? Everyone – agreeing on the brilliance of this solution – looked at me. By now I was far too wise in the ways of the Commission – and mindful of my responsibilities as a professional accountant – to fall for that one.

I stressed that we needed to focus on basic problems. "At the moment the current system doesn't provide the Chief Accountant with the necessary information to sign off such accounts."

Crucially, I also pointed out that it would eventually have to be my predecessor who would have to sign off the 2001 accounts – as I had joined only in 2002. And I added, "I haven't yet received the statement of account on handover that is standard in any organization."

During that same meeting I was informed that I would have to go to the Budget Committee of the Council of Ministers for the presentation of the new Financial Regulation that was being drafted. I replied that I had not yet been given the chance of reviewing or commenting on the draft. "But I have heard that they have eliminated certain important controls and that worries me."

Silence and a change of subject were the only immediate

response to my point. But later Maison made it clear that not only did he not want me interfering in any of his plans for 'reform' embodied in the new Financial Regulation, but that he wanted me to be the one to present it to the Council of Ministers. If there was any gunfire, I would be the one in the front line!

In later meetings on this issue, I found out that while the new regulation was promised for January 2003, the new accounting system needed for its implementation was going to be available only in 2005. At this point, I could only repeat my earlier concerns that the Directors General would never assume responsibility for their respective budgets unless we provided them with a system that produced reliable figures. I also repeated the dangers of weakening the traditional controls the Chief Accountant had before authorizing payments.

"The Chief Accountant remains the person ultimately responsible for the assets and monies entrusted to the European Union – and therefore has to check the supporting documentation before releasing EU funds. I know of no other organization in the world where the treasurer makes payments without seeing the invoices."

My comments were not well received and I sensed a growing general nervousness about my appearance before the Council of Ministers' Budget Committee. The following day I was called to a meeting with fellow Director Jacques Mon who had clearly been deputed to coach me in what needed to be said and not said at that meeting. He was the Director with whom I had had most contact when being initiated into my job and was in charge of drafting the new Financial Regulation.

In our discussions, I still found it scarcely credible that, after the debacle of the Santer Commission, more power over EU funds was being given to the Directors General, at the same time as providing them with a perfect excuse for evading responsibility: the unreliability of the accounting system. I wondered how the Council of Ministers and the European Parliament would react to this – particularly as some MEPs appeared to have some notion of the seriousness of the situation and they had the power to press for a solution.

At the Council meeting, Mon spoke at length. There was some flak from those who could follow what he was saying about the new Financial Regulation, to be introduced in 2003, being implemented on a new accounting system promised for two years later.

For my part, being under strict instructions about what to say, and still feeling new to the job, I restricted myself to some fairly anodyne additional points about how the new rules would affect financial reports – and the way in which they managed these matters in the private sector. But I wondered whether I would look back on this meeting as a great opportunity missed – as a time when I should have at least attempted to bring home to the EU's political masters just how far short the new regulation was falling from the proper management of EU funds.

Before my first month was up, I was involved in one more area of conflict: the European Development Fund. The fund was separate from the EU budget as not all member states contributed to it and there was no pre-determined budget for the year. Its operation had little in common with the EU general budget, as it had a different accounting system – and its staff felt happy and proud about its functioning.

When Maison proposed merging it into the EU general budget, I thought it made little sense to merge something that was working relatively well with something that quite clearly wasn't. But as so often with the Commission, there was more to this matter than first met the eye.

CHAPTER III

EXPRESSING MY VIEWS

From the beginning of February 2002, I came under increasing pressure from Mon over the signing off of the 2001 accounts. Essentially, despite my misgivings expressed at meetings with Maison, he wanted my signature on the 2001 accounts which were to be sent out to the Directors General for them to sign their 'annual declarations.' Given the impossibility of coming up with one coherent set of accounts from the computer system, and as I had joined the Commission only in the previous month, I had no intention of providing my signature.

"The signature you need is that of my predecessor," I insisted. When Mon suggested meetings in an effort to sort the matter out, I pointed out that the person who really needed to be there was my predecessor.

By now, I had established who this was – and he was not the one, intimated at my September 11 interview, who had taken sick and died. That was the predecessor of my predecessor. My real predecessor – Paul Lematin* – was actually alive and well and still working for the Commission's research centre, ISPRA, in Italy. He was the one who, as director of resources and a head of unit, should have been there at my first grim meeting in Varese.

When I had first tackled Maison on the subject of my predecessor, he had had a slightly different story, again vague, about Lematin going through "a messy divorce .." and wanting to get away from Brussels. But that didn't ring true either. If he were a family man, surely he would want to stay somewhere near his children. My own growing suspicion was that he had wanted to get out of Brussels to get away from a messy set of accounts.

When I spoke with Lematin at ISPRA I found him, over the course of an hour, to be studiously vague. Every specific question was met with sonorous declarations on the need to trust your colleagues, the work they do and the figures that they produce.

Wearily, I reminded Mon, "I have not yet received a proper statement of account on the official handover of the job." And indeed, I never did.

In the weekly meetings with my staff, I realized that some of them grasped these issues only too well. Some mentioned that the precise role and independence of the Chief Accountant had always been a matter of some uncertainty and controversy within the Budget Directorate. They could see that implementation of the new Financial Regulation – sending out accounts signed by the Chief Accountant to the Directors General – would make that role even less clear. They appeared alarmed that my predecessor had still not drawn up a statement of account on transferring his responsibilities to me.

While I was still trying to resolve these issues, documents kept on arriving in my office for signature while answers to my questions kept on being more and more delayed. I worked late into the night trying to sort out the mounds of inadequate paperwork. Looking up the rules in my office, I usually found them perfectly sound. Too often they were simply not being followed.

I had a steady barrage of questions for staff in my Treasury unit: Who is the beneficiary we are paying this money to? For what purpose? Do we have any proof that the work was done? Where is this covered in the budget? Why does the EU delegation in this country need three separate current accounts?

As time went on, it was difficult not to see the European Union as being like an open cash till in a shop – just waiting to be robbed.

Meanwhile, the issue of the unsigned 2001 accounts refused to go away. Calls from Mon were getting more frequent. In one in which he pressed for my signature, I again offered to attend a meeting on the issue as long as Lematin was also present.

At this point Mon told me that I would not last long in the European Commission if I did not comply with the instructions of the Director General (Maison.) I reminded him of my independence as Chief Accountant and he hung up.

This was the first open warning I had received – and I did not feel happy at someone attempting to coerce me in my job.

At the next Directors' meeting, I got the impression that Maison had been fully briefed by Mon about our recent disagreement. Maison immediately started lecturing me about what he saw as my responsibility in the annual declarations. I asked to be given the opportunity to detail in professional terms the situation we were facing.

Once again, I explained about the unreliability of the accounting system, the importance of the institution's accounts, and the responsibility of the Chief Accountant to make sure they were correct. I stressed the accountability of each person involved in drawing up the accounts – and the difficulty of ensuring that accountability with such a fundamentally flawed computer system. To myself, I wondered how many more times we could keep on going over the same old ground.

All listened in silence. At the end of my speech, Maison commented that this was the first time that the Commission had a Chief Accountant who was a qualified accountant. He said he was beginning to learn, as would our colleagues.

Later, I was even congratulated by one of my fellow Directors on the robustness of my stand. Could this be the beginning of a new era .. a new dawn?

Alas, not. In the days which followed I realized that I might as well have saved my breath. Though there were a series of meetings, chaired by Deputy Director General Jens Mogen, to consider my points, they never ended with any specific plan of action. Any proposals I made for new computer systems – even those needed on the grounds of direst necessity – were waved away on account of "budget limitations."

When I again raised these issues at the next Directors' meeting, I was told of a report from the Court of Auditors – which I had not yet seen. Maison had and was reported to be disgusted with its contents. I asked to have a copy – and was told that it had already been sent to my office.

With Maison alone, I took the opportunity of mentioning, again, the need for my predecessor to produce a proper handover document, with a signed statement of account, and was airily invited to sort the matter out with his assistant Theodor Lemercier. He in turn informed me, point blank, that the financial regulations did not provide for any such statement to be presented on the change of accountant and that, if my predecessor agreed to do so, it would only be "out of good will".

Later, reading up on the fine detail of the financial regulation in my own office, I found that in fact they did. Back I returned to Maison's office with the relevant volume – only to be met with the Euro-equivalent of a Gallic shrug.

Increasingly, over the next few weeks I developed a sense of not always being given the correct information, the necessary documents – and of being kept slightly out of the loop. I also got a feeling that more of my staff were sitting on the fence. Some of my senior subordinates had clearly known that, from the start, I was not Maison's choice for the job, and the more sympathetic mentioned battles fought by Maison with the predecessor who came before Lematin.

Others still clearly worshipped their Director General. One even rhapsodized to me about the way in which Maison, at one meeting of the Council of Ministers, had banged his fist on the table to emphasize a point.

Some might have interpreted such behavior as either bad manners or the sign of a person with a poor argument. But I had already become aware that banging the table and yelling was quite often part of the bag of tricks deployed to flex muscles in the upper echelons of the Commission.

My own rule was never to raise my voice, to use arguments based on facts and rational thought and, above all, seek the advice of others. In my meetings with my staff, I couldn't help being aware that growing numbers were becoming more non-committal in their advice – and a touch less warm and supportive.

In any forthcoming head-on collision between Maison and myself, it was natural that people should start manoeuvering to line up with the winner – and for growing numbers that appeared not to be me.

In his 13 years in the job, Maison had certainly acquired awesome savvy and awesome clout – as had his long-serving Spanish counterpart, Pedro Laguna*, who was Director General for Agriculture. In most organizations, it would have been a basic, common-sense control to rotate people in such critical positions. But they served on – a Frenchman and a Spaniard who came from the two countries which enjoyed by far and away the most generous portions of subsidies from the 100-billion Euro budget.

Would Commissioner Schreyer be any help in pushing through badly needed reforms? Each week, she held a meeting with Maison and the Directors, where most of the matters discussed were "political." But as political affairs often have a financial aspect, I always tried to attend – even when not specifically invited. At first, I made little or no comments. Simply being there turned out to be highly revealing of what actually happened at Commissioner level.

Each Commissioner had a half-a-dozen-strong cabinet headed by an all-powerful Chef de Cabinet – a civil servant of equivalent Grade 2 level to myself. In Schreyer's case this was a tall, grey-haired fellow-German Hans Zimmer* – and he appeared to have the traditional iron grip on information going before his Commissioner boss.

To prepare myself for one meeting - where the outcome of the budget for 2001 was going to be discussed – I decided to pull out the final figures for the budget that was actually spent. This was one area where I felt I had expertise and could possibly contribute to the discussion.

But as the meeting itself progressed I was stunned to realize that Schreyer's figures and mine simply didn't mesh. According to my research, I could see that at the end of 2001 the under-expenditure was 15 billion euros – 10 billion euros more than the 5 billion figure the Commissioner appeared to be reading in her reports. This was an error of more than ten per cent of the total annual budget at that time.

This simply didn't jell with Maison's description, in some meetings, of a Commissioner who was something of a control freak and as a person who got rather too obsessed with the details of issues. In point of fact, she had already been in the job, and presumably followed the budget, for two years, and yet didn't appear to have noticed that some 10 billion euros had gone walkabout.

"Where does the Commissioner get her figures from?" I asked

my staff when I got back to my office. They explained that whereas in the past, financial reports would be distributed in hard copy, Schreyer's cabinet had instructed the Accounting Services to send reports directly to them via e-mail – so no one could be sure that the Commissioner had got to see the figures actually produced by our department.

To me, it was fairly obvious that the figures and reports were pretty well cooked before they ever reached the Commissioner's desk. The matter of over or under-expenditure was clearly a matter of key importance in the negotiation of the final budget for the new year in the European Parliament and Council of Ministers. Why should the Member States be endlessly asked to cough up even more money? Yet it appeared that the Commissioner in charge of the department was not being given the true figures.

On another occasion, one of my unit heads brought me a question asked by a Member of the European Parliament, who wanted to know how much money had been recovered from the overpayment of agricultural funds over the previous five years. Knowing that the Commission kept no central record of such payments – nor did it do any follow-up research – I could only truthfully answer that it was impossible to come up with a true figure.

But nobody appeared unduly worried at this revelation – or what it said about the manifest lack of control of EU funds. All they were really worried about was getting this particular MEP off their backs so that they could move on. More of my staff's time was thus wasted as the query circulated through various sections until a barely honest answer had been honed into a state of almost perfect obscurity.

On this same issue, towards the end of February, the head of my Recoveries unit, Helmut Herr*, contacted me to let me know that Schreyer's cabinet head Zimmer had asked him to explain a report that he had produced. Herr was concerned that his report covered only ten per cent of the budget – that part relating to direct payments made by the Commission to beneficiaries or suppliers – and that the Commissioner's office might want to use this methodology as a means of explaining a recovery process for the whole budget.

Once again, I was surprised that a subordinate, and head of unit, had been invited to get involved in all this without my being informed, and decided to go along with him. On my advice, Herr explained to the Commissioner the truth about the unreliability of the data we had produced and the fact that it covered only "direct payments" – some ten per cent of budget.

In fact, I saw this meeting with the Commissioner as the perfect opportunity for bringing home to her not just this but so many other glaring shortcomings in the system. I had not yet had the chance of speaking with her on her own. When my colleague had finished his explanations, I remained seated. "Commissioner, I wonder whether I could have a word with you alone."

As this was entirely against the "culture" of the place, Zimmer left the room with evident reluctance and ill grace. Clearly, Commissioners were very rarely left on their own – without the "guidance" of either their cabinets or all-powerful Directors General.

But I was determined to take advantage of this opportunity. "I am extremely worried about the computer system on which the funds are managed." She admitted that she too had received a lot of complaints – but that she was waiting for a report from the Court of Auditors on an audit done in 2001.

"What do you suggest?" she asked. I told her of the possibility of expanding the use of a well-known German software package, with a customized version which had already been bought by the Commission but was not being used. "That would solve many of the biggest problems."

Further, I mentioned a report from the Court of Auditors that had come in and that I had not yet had time to read. She asked for a copy. She was keen on using the German software – but wanted to see the auditors' report, presumably confirming the failure of the existing system, to make it more difficult for others to argue against her view.

Back in my office, I saw the Court of Auditors' report that I had mentioned was in French – which Schreyer didn't speak. I rang her to tell her that – and she asked me to get a translation. The Court of Auditors informed me that translating the whole 80-page report would take a long time – but they agreed to translate its main conclusions which were later sent to the Commissioner.

I was tempted to believe that my meeting with Schreyer had been a real breakthrough – that at last the basic problems of her directorate would be tackled. But as more time went by, I could see the difficulties and weakness of her position. A political appointee, she clearly felt she had to fit in with political decisions and go with the flow of the College of Commissioners. Nobody had ever argued that the member states were sending their finest and brightest to be senior politicians in Brussels. Understandably, the smartest stayed at home – and tried to become Prime Minister.

Most of these political appointees, who ended up as Commissioners in Brussels, were there for just one five-year term. Unless they were people of quite exceptional intelligence and determination, they were no match for the Directors General and cabinet heads who had often worked in the Commission for years and knew, like no other bureaucracy in the world, how to arrange agendas, sift documents and stuff diaries with time-wasting nonsense.

For my own part, I was beginning to see that my own independence as Chief Accountant – in theory directly responsible to the College of Commissioners – could be something of a myth. Never again did Zimmer risk leaving me alone with Commissioner Schreyer. Invariably, Maison or someone else was conjured onto the scene.

More clearly than before, I could see that the very description of my job as both Accounting Officer and Budget Execution Director was something of an anomaly as both posts covered pretty much the same responsibilities. But the nomination of Budget Execution Director craftily enforced my reporting to Budget Director General Maison. I now knew that I had a battle on my hands.

Meanwhile, back in Varese, Lematin continued to drag his feet. He simply refused to take responsibility for signing the 2001 accounts to be sent out to the Directors General for their annual declaration. I could now see why he had moved out of the Chief Accountant's job after less than one year on the job. I was also beginning to realize that, while Maison clearly did not want me for the job, he had possibly accepted my nomination in the hope that a newcomer could be bounced into signing the accounts – before knowing what was really going on.

But that hadn't worked. The situation was now becoming tense. Complaints were coming in daily from the various Directorates about figures in the computer system not matching those they had put in.

Finally, Maison announced to all the Directorates that the Budget Directorate General would "underpin" the accounts sent to them for their annual declarations. I wondered how the Director General could support accounts that the Chief Accountant refused to sign. But I argued no more – as I still hoped to make the most necessary changes to improve the situation in the shortest possible time.

At the next Directors' meeting Maison asked me to resolve the issue of the reduction of my staff that he had promised for that year's budget. I pointed out the existing lack of trained personnel in the Accounting services. Ignoring my point, he retorted that that was always the complaint of my staff – which was particularly absurd when they hadn't even filled the vacant posts.

At that same meeting, Maison mentioned the report on the financial systems that had just been produced by the Court of Auditors (the AMIS report: Audit of Management and Information Systems). He strongly dismissed its criticisms indicating that the language used was quite extraordinary – intemperate. Others joined in with a chorus of disapproval and disgust – apart from myself. I found I couldn't disagree with the auditors' conclusions – but kept quiet, not wanting to start yet another argument. Already, though, I could see the report causing many headaches in the weeks to come.

By now I had been to countless meetings at which I had tried to explain the failings of the system – and to propose solutions. But most of these gatherings ended up with no decisions being taken and much hand-wringing about "budget limitations." Again and again, I tried to explain that my proposals would not necessarily involve massive investment – but mainly further and better use of the computer software that was already to hand.

Increasingly, I felt myself to be in an Alice in Wonderland world – with what was now being discussed as 'reform' simply making the situation worse. In the future, the Directors General would pretty much control the funds and if any "irregularity" were found, the Commissioners would blame the Directors General who would in turn blame an inadequate accounting system – and so on, round and round in an almost perfect circle of irresponsibility!

Already, both Commissioners and Directors General were happy to heap much of the blame for "irregularities" onto member states, where 75 per cent of the money is spent on agricultural subsidies and structural funds. They were equally happy to overlook the fact that, even if the money is passed on, it is still the responsibility of the Commission to insist on the documentation from its eventual recipients to show that the funds have been spent properly. Indeed, the Treaties emphasize that it is the European Commission which is responsible for all the EU funds.

I couldn't help wondering why we, the European taxpayers, should go on forever handing enormous sums to an organization – the European Commission – which refused (and still refuses) to take any responsibility for looking after them.

Often I wondered whether much had changed at all since the collapse of the Jacques Santer Commission when the "Wise Men" had reported that it had been "particularly difficult to find anyone who has the slightest sense of responsibility."

CHAPTER IV

THE PRESSURE TO
SIGN INCREASES

At the start of March I was informed of a meeting, scheduled for April 18, at which I would have to present a draft of my proposals for the accounting reform. This meeting would be with the President of the Court of Auditors – Juan Manuel Fabra Valles – and two other directors responsible for the annual report.

But I pointed out, "To present a proper action plan, we have got to sort out not only the accounting framework but also the computer system we propose to use. In order to do that, Mon and those in charge of the computer system will have to present their proposals to me so that I can combine the two bits of information."

At about that same time I received a call from Schreyer's office asking if I could have my proposals on the accounting reform ready for the end of May. At first sight this seemed a not unreasonable request, until I was informed that, once my draft was prepared, it would need 'inter-service' consultation within the Commission's other Directorates, and translation into other languages – a process that would take at least a month.

In effect, if the finished report had been scheduled (before my arrival) for the end of March, they were giving me just two months, since taking up my employment, in which to prepare it. In view of all my other responsibilities, this presented me with an impossible timetable, if anything of value was going to be produced.

Also during March, the Court of Auditors' AMIS report – on the Audit of Management and Information Systems – came back for discussion. Maison wanted all four of his Directors to respond to each point in the report. "From my own experience," I pointed out, "I can confirm that all the essential points raised by the Auditors are correct." Immediately, I was contradicted by Maison, who was backed up by the other Directors.

Once again, I was on my own. I tried to explain that, "The only way of starting reform is to recognize the existence and size of a problem." As I spoke I was reminded of Jules Muis's comment to me of the " Commission living within a culture of self-denial."

I also went on to point out that as my predecessor was the one who was in charge when the audit was done – (and the report had serious criticisms of him) – he should be the one to respond to its points. But I offered to indicate the areas on which I felt we should focus – and later sent an e-mail, outlining them, to Maison.

Two days later, on March 6, when I was in Luxembourg, I was called by Maison about my reluctance to contradict the auditors and by his tone I realized that the criticisms contained within the AMIS report had far more importance for him than I had at first thought.

The reason that I was in Luxembourg was in itself significant. A few days before that, on March 4, I had come back from lunch in Brussels to be informed by my secretary that, just five minutes earlier, Deputy DG Mogen had been in my office with Mr Juan Barco*, who had taken over Pierre Sachet's job as a director of the Court of Auditors in charge of the EU budget. He would be the one with whom I was likely to have most dealings in the future.

I was surprised. Mogen had made no mention of Barco's visit when I had spoken with him a few days earlier – let alone invited me to join him in a meeting.

When he got back to Luxembourg, Barco rang to express his regrets that we had not met as there were important issues he wanted to discuss with me. Embarrassed by all this, I offered to travel to Luxembourg and meet with him in the next day or so. It was difficult now to avoid the impression that deliberate efforts were being made to hamper my contacts with the Auditors. Though I apologized for some "crossing of wires," I could tell that Barco also found it hard to believe that such a misunderstanding had been accidental. He faxed me a letter that eloquently summed up the Auditors' concerns, and I was intrigued by the fact that they so clearly regarded me as the principal player in sorting out the mess.

When I met him in Luxembourg, Barco continued his onslaught on the Budget Directorate, and said I needed to do something about the 2001 accounts. "I'm afraid it's a bit late, but I'll do my best," I replied.

Barco informed me that if the accounts did not show real progress over those of the previous year the Court might refuse clearance altogether. He said it was that bad. He acknowledged that I had a difficult job, and I stressed that his support as an auditor was crucial if I were to succeed in reforming the accounting.

"My predecessor still hasn't handed over any statement of account since my arrival – and though I have asked for it, he has simply ignored my requests," I pointed out. "Better send him a warning letter," Barco suggested. I did so that same day.

On my return from Luxembourg, I asked for a meeting with Maison. First of all, I wanted to sort out the issues in the

Auditors' AMIS report that had sparked his electric telephone call. "As a professional accountant, I simply can't deny the points that the Court of Auditors are making." I also wanted to pass on the warning that the court might refuse clearance of the 2001 accounts altogether.

Although I was not technically responsible for the 2001 accounts, I repeated my offer to do what I could to help improve them. The most urgent need was for a 'reconciliation' of the accounts – combining data from different sources - which had never been done before. Further, I tried to impress on him the desperate lack of people in my team with a reasonable knowledge of accounting.

To keep costs down, I offered to take on consultants on a temporary basis. Maison was non-committal. Later that same day, I met with Luc Montagne*, the Directorate's head of resources who immediately put a limit on my request for staff – both for the urgent needs of the 2001 accounts and the long-term demands of the accounting reforms. And, indeed, I heard nothing more on the subject.

Still worried about the quality of the 2001 accounts, and the fact that Schreyer would be adopting them on behalf of the whole Commission by the end of April, I asked for a meeting with her which her office confirmed for a week later: on March 18. Over the weekend, I prepared a short note listing the points I wanted to discuss which I sent to her before the meeting.

Around that time, I was contacted by one of Maison's staff asking me to request the Auditors to delete paragraph 102 of their AMIS report. But the paragraph was of fundamental importance as it basically stated that, given the quality of the accounting systems, it was impossible for the Accounting Officer to present reliable accounts.

Clearly, Maison was infuriated by the implication that the Court of Auditors would never be able to give a clean bill of health to the accounts – unless the computer system was changed. It seemed hardly fair to make this request of me knowing that fact to be true and knowing my responsibility for the current year accounts. I could only reply that, "As an accounting professional I cannot properly make that request. Only the Director General, using his political power, can make such a request."

I was finding it difficult to understand why Maison and his team were still making such efforts to resist such obvious reforms. Evidence of the failure of the current system was being revealed almost daily.

Crucially, there was an investigation into Eurostat – a Luxembourg-based agency which, among other things, publishes statistics used for determining the contributions of member states and the subsidies to be paid out. Some of the work is done by outside companies. Eurostat also sells statistics to private companies. In all this operation, there had long been suspicions of fraudulent trading.

Indeed, an investigation that had been going on since 1997 seemed to illustrate perfectly the points I had been trying to make about the Commission's lack of proper controls. It was alleged that during the 1990s, Eurostat officials had used a double accounting system to transfer large amounts of money to secret bank accounts not monitored by auditors and that the value of some contracts was being grossly inflated. At the very least, it was suspected that between four and six million euros had been "siphoned off" in this way.

It was only as the result of some very determined prodding by some brave Commission officials and aggrieved contractors that OLAF – the European Anti-Fraud Office – and the Internal Audit Directorate were eventually galvanized into action. But their difficulty in tracing the sums of money, and the principals and possible beneficiaries involved, was precisely because of the lack of an electronic audit trail that I had been warning about since my arrival in office. I had some contact with OLAF in mid-March, 2002, on a different issue – and received little assurance as to the speed and vigour with which their investigations were likely to proceed.

That meeting – with Maison, the head of OLAF and the head of the Legal service – was ostensibly to work out the varying responsibilities of the different services on the recovery of unaccounted funds. But as so often – with the EU's morass of competing and contradictory laws – the meeting was a complete mess, with each of the principals trying to load responsibility onto somebody else.

My only contribution was to point out that, "Whatever is decided, under the EU treaties the Chief Accountant remains solely responsible for all assets and monies of the EU, and I cannot shift this responsibility onto whomsoever else I find suitable. That is the law. "

In the end, nothing was decided. The head of the Legal service issued one minute of the meeting, Maison another. Neither, as far as I know, was ever made official – and the whole exercise was fairly typical of daily life in the Commission.

Next up, that same day, was a Budget Directorate meeting on "Internal Control Standards," at which I was shocked to hear that the Treasury function was not considered an area of risk. As this is the department responsible for the safe collection and disbursement of funds, I had to point out, "In my view, the Treasury function is an area of fundamental risk throughout the entire European Union and requires urgent attention."

But Maison insisted that the significance of the EU Treasury function was minor. I could not help comparing the EU to a bank that takes in and pays out money – adding no other value beyond the proper control of those funds. Despite the fact that this was the essential activity of the Commission, it had been an area of almost total failure.

I took the opportunity to point out that during the ten weeks I had been in the job I had been meeting regularly with the head of my Treasury unit, Charles Cash, to discuss the controls on payments and bank accounts, and for details on specific transactions I was being asked to authorize.

I did not spell out that the delay in answering queries – and his failure to produce a list of signatories authorized to approve payments – could in no way be considered reasonable.

On the day I was to meet with Schreyer – March 18 – another important meeting, with the Auditors to discuss their AMIS report, had been scheduled for one hour earlier. While Maison had announced the AMIS meeting that morning, he had made no reference to any meeting with Schreyer. Neither did I, still believing that my discussion would be with her alone. Wrong!

As the time for me to see Schreyer came close, I said I had to leave the AMIS meeting – and so did Maison. And I next saw him storming up the stairs ahead of me towards the Commissioner's office. When I got there, I found him already installed in Schreyer's office with cabinet head Hans Zimmer.

While this simply confirmed for me the extent to which Commissioners could be manipulated and cocooned by the Commission bureaucracy, I was nevertheless determined to reveal the inadequacy of the 2001 accounts which Schreyer was intending to adopt at the end of April.

But no sooner had I opened my mouth than the two men interrupted to argue that all the points I was making related to the accounting reform that I had to put in place. Patiently, I countered that there were two separate issues. "First, there is the problem of improving the 2001 accounts in the month and a half that is left and being aware of their shortcomings. Secondly, there are the deficiencies of the current accounting system and judging the extent to which the suggested proposals are likely to change them."

Once again, I spoke of the need for a fully integrated system that would allow the processing of transactions to feed the necessary ledgers so as to allow a permanent and continuous reconciliation of the budget and of outgoing payments. There was little interest in what I was saying. Eventually, Schreyer asked me for a written description of the problem, consequences and proposals for action, and, with that the meeting ended.

For me, the real significance of the meeting was that I was beginning to realize that the Commissioner who had hired me against enormous opposition – and probably with the intention of bringing about real change – was about to throw in the towel. Unwilling to rock the boat, she was now allowing herself to be manipulated. I couldn't help but contrast the whole tone of this meeting with the one I had had a month earlier – when I had spoken with her on her own.

After that meeting of March 18 I noticed a couple of my senior subordinates beginning to adopt positions likely to block my suggestions. Whereas earlier they had given the impression of being open to new ideas, most discussions now concluded with their suggesting that we stick to proposals that had been drafted a year earlier – and with no variations.

And yet, they were able to give me no good reason as to why they had already waited a year to implement reforms that they believed to be so sound. By now it was pretty obvious that they were falling in with Maison's strategy of imposing his own reforms – under the signature of the new Chief Accountant.

To me, however, Maison's proposed changes to what was referred to as the new Financial Regulation – the relevant EU law – were deeply flawed. While earlier, many of my colleagues had privately admitted that they had long known that the system lacked coherence, security and comprehensiveness, I could see that what was now being discussed as "reform" would only make the situation worse.

For in giving more power to the Directors General to approve projects and order payments, I realized that there would be a further weakening of the existing inadequate checks on invoices and contracts and efforts to verify the amount, purpose and beneficiary of a payment. For the Directors General this would bring more power – but the responsibility for error would remain mine.

Meanwhile, on March 20, the Court of Auditors had alerted me to serious anomalies they had found in the Commission's 'SINCOM' computer system which, in their words, would ".. seriously impact on the accounts for 2001." Again, I was intrigued that they had brought the problem directly to me – clearly seeing me as having overall responsibility for the computer systems on which financial transactions were processed: the very area where Maison had been trying to strip me of authority.

What particularly bothered the Court was the fact that unauthorized people could get onto that computer system, add, delete or change transactions and log off – leaving no electronic trail.

I copied their note to Maison to let him know what was going on – and also forwarded the letter to Schreyer – in the hope that she might still promote the use of the German software package that we had discussed in our previous, private meeting. Contrary to what its opponents claimed, it would have required no extra investment, as it had been purchased five years earlier, and had already been customized for the EU. I had checked that we already had all the licenses needed for its full operation.

Given the Auditors' concerns, and with the continuing lack of response to so many of my questions to the Treasury unit, and, crucially, their failure to produce a list of those with signing authority, I finally felt I had no alternative but to request an independent audit of the whole Treasury function.

One had not been done for ten years – and the unit clearly played a crucial role with its gathering and handing out of funds.

I discussed the issue with Maison and we agreed (or so I thought) that I would request such an audit from the Internal Audit Directorate as soon as possible. No sooner had that been done than I heard from Maison's office that they would do the audit.

I stressed to Maison that, "The audit has to be done by a Directorate completely separate from that to which our Treasury unit is attached. The whole point of the audit is that it should be seen to be independent."

To no avail. Maison's office duly dispatched a letter to Internal Audit informing them that his team would do the audit. The task, they claimed, was already in their programme of work for 2002. (Later, I discovered that it had been added only when I requested the audit.)

Gradually, I could see that my request for a Treasury audit was causing massive unease. I saw it as something that any of the big private international accounting firms could accomplish in a couple of weeks. But I also knew, as they knew, that such an audit might raise questions about the Commission as the guardian of EU funds and about the competence and actions of specific civil servants who had held responsibility for 15 or 20 years.

My suspicions were simply strengthened when conversations with Zimmer and other senior officials revealed a streak of near-paranoia about my audit request. "Who is it that is putting you up to this, Marta? What outside group are you working for? Who sent you here?"

Their suspicions were clearly absurd. If I had been connected with any outside political group this would surely have been revealed in the pre-recruitment checks that I knew had been done on me. They had spoken to at least three people at the OECD.

All in all, it was being made crystal clear that Director General Maison had absolutely no long-term intention of respecting my independence, or judgement, as Chief Accountant. With the time that he and Treasury unit head, Charles Cash, had spent in their jobs – more than 12 years each – and their adamant refusal to supply me with crucial information, or allow a truly independent audit of their operations, I could come to no other conclusion.

Tension in the office was becoming palpable. I decided to take two days off to finalise my installation in Brussels. As I had agreed to transfer to the city in just two weeks, I had still not had time to really sort out my personal life. I had had to go flat-hunting in my lunch time as the working days had been going on for so long. I had had to research the possibility of my daughter Carolina going to school in Brussels, and make arrangements for my husband to spend time with me there.

When I got back to the office, on March 25, I discovered that my participation in the visit to the Court of Auditors, in Luxembourg, scheduled for April 18, had evidently been cancelled – given the disappearance of my name from the official documentation.

Maison had instructed my subordinates to finalise a document that he could explain to the Auditors himself. This, despite the fact that the Deputy DG Mogen had already informed me that I would be needed on the trip to discuss the accounting reforms.

I e-mailed Maison expressing surprise at the cancellation, and to make sure that I had got that right. Instantly, he was on the phone telling me that he was not going to allow me to dictate whom he should or should not take to a meeting. I pointed out that it was obvious and natural that the Chief Accountant should be the one to present accounting reforms. I also reminded him that when I had discussed the draft June 2001 reforms with the Court of Auditors, they had taken the line that as they had not been presented to them officially by the then Accounting Officer (Lematin) they had seen no reason for an official reaction. "Above all, the Auditors have indicated that they are now far more interested in seeing action – rather than draft projects."

Maison simply upped the pressure in making life difficult. He instructed me to take on all the extra responsibilities of accounting being transferred from ISPRA, in Italy, as well as to find jobs for those losing theirs in Varese – but without any extra personnel.

By now, I realized that much of the power of the Budget Director General – and his ability to frustrate reforms – derived from his control over manpower. Before I had joined, Maison had proposed substantial staff cuts for the Accounting services in his budget for the year – but none for his own area of responsibility.

As time went on, I became aware of more of my subordinates positioning themselves for any imminent battle for power. The most explicit example of this came when, at the beginning of April, Mara Villos, with whom I had been working most closely on the reform proposals, suddenly indicated that she would not be able to sign the final document. It differed, she claimed, from the original version that we had been proposing.

None of this had been mentioned in the preceding weeks, as we had been grinding our way through succeeding versions. In reality, there had not been any major changes. When I invited her to put her complaint, and what she saw as the discrepancies, in writing, she backed down. There had been a "misunderstanding," she explained.

That same afternoon we presented the proposals to Maison, who gave no immediate reaction. But when I informed him that I would be sending a more extensive document about the accounting reforms to Schreyer, as she had requested in our meeting with her of March 18, he objected.

He argued that, for that particular document, any computer system changes should also be included, and that – in clear contradiction of Treaty rules – it was his staff who had to be responsible for such changes. He told me that Mon was also working on proposals at that moment. But they never materialised.

Indeed, Mon himself didn't even bother to turn up when the issue was again discussed at the next weekly Directors' meeting. All that emerged was continuing opposition to my suggestion to expand the use of the German software which the EU had already bought. Others claimed that it was the Directors General who did not want to use the German software as they found it "too complex."

I pointed out, again, that, "It is the Directors General who are now regularly complaining about the existing system, as the figures they put in do not correspond with the ones they get out. Perfectly correctly, they are pointing out that the control of funds is impossible." It seemed to be an argument that could go on forever – even if it was in reality unarguable.

More to the point, I had by now established that Maison's assertion that his staff should control the computer system was flatly wrong. The EU's Financial Regulation and Treaties gave the Chief Accountant absolute power to approve the financial systems ".. on which the transactions that affect the EU budget .." were processed. This meant that control over the entire system, including the ones used in the different Directorates, was in my hands.

Yet Maison's regard for the rules remained wholly elastic. I had often been appalled when temporary consultants, fellow enarques and protégés of Maison, were present when confidential matters were discussed. On one occasion, when a particularly delicate issue was to be broached, I had intimated to Maison that the temporary consultant should leave.

Maison exploded saying that never in his career had he faced a similar situation and who did I think I was to put such request to him. But I stood firm. I told Maison, "This is an issue that I believe that we should discuss only with Directors." Eventually, the temporary official and Maison's assistant left the room.

As we were now nearing mid-April – even though the reform project was not finalized – I wrote to all the Directors General announcing that I would be conducting an inventory of the financial transactions in each Directorate to determine the needs of the new accounting system.

The very next day, Maison called an urgent meeting to discuss a letter from Martin Berry*, the Director General for Enlargement of the EU. In it he announced that he was considering putting reservations, in his annual declaration "on those matters which are the responsibility of the Budget Director General and therefore outside my control."

Translated into simple language, this said that he was refusing to take responsibility for figures coming from an accounting system that he did not think was reliable.

Panic. Maison had clearly been anxious about just such a reaction – but had hoped to clear it by saying that the Chief Accountant would sign the accounts sent to the Directorates. Given my refusal to do so, he had a problem.

Maison took some time to react and finally informed Berry that he would be "expressing reservations on the accounting system and controls .." in his own declaration.

This gave me the opportunity of repeating my own proposals for urgent reforms – and remind Maison that I was still waiting for Mon's suggestions on the computer systems to send with my document to the Commissioner.

Later, I went to see Berry myself. Given the reservations he had so clearly expressed about the workings of the new Financial Regulation, I saw him as someone who possibly understood the weaknesses of the whole system and would be prepared to support me in making the necessary changes – and therefore was a possible future ally. Wrong.

In my meeting with him, it soon became clear that all he was really interested in was in making sure that no responsibility stuck to him for his participation in what was obviously an unreliable system – and not to sign the annual declaration required of him with Maison's proposed changes.

A workshop on risk assessment brought back the issue of the Treasury audit, where Maison firmly spelt out that it would be done by his staff and by no one outside his department. He again stressed that he felt that the Treasury function at the EU was minimal – and therefore not an area of risk. While all others agreed with him, I insisted, "The Treasury function is absolutely crucial in an organization such as the Commission."

That same day I received a copy of a letter sent by Maison to Jules Muis, Director General of Internal Audit, in which he firmly rebuffed Muis's concerns about the Commission's Treasury accounting. The document was about the most cynical and arrogant I was to read during my time at the Commission. In plain language, Maison was basically saying that he didn't really care about controls of the accounting system. He cared only about the political consequences when his directorate was criticized by the European Parliament – at which point he would certainly fight his corner.

This was veteran Maison informing relative newcomer Muis that the whole thing was really just a game of power – in Maison's words an "inter-institutional game" between Parliament and Commission. Given the supine way in which the Parliament had, year after year – and despite the reservations of the Court of Auditors – continued to approve the accounts, it was possible to see how Maison could have dared to commit such cynicism to paper. But where the EU taxpayer fitted into any of this was of course omitted.

After the risk assessment workshop, a meeting was called by Maison to discuss preparations for the April 18 visit to the Court of Auditors. As I arrived in his office, I found that he had also invited Mara Villos, the person with whom I had been working most closely on the reform project.

With almost studied rudeness, Maison ignored my presence throughout the entire meeting and referred all his questions to Villos. And still he failed to make it clear whether I would be needed on the trip to Luxembourg to make the presentation. His behavior, in fact, was becoming so uncouth that I wondered whether he was trying to provoke me into some kind of retaliatory insult or action. His manners seemed to be reaching for some new low in human arrogance.

But I forced myself to remain calm and stay to the end of the meeting. If nothing else, it served to confirm that he was now using my staff to block my proposals.

In the light of recent events – and Maison's apparent refusal to take on board any of my warnings or suggestions about the accounting system – I decided to write directly to Commissioner Schreyer. First, I wanted to reiterate my suggestion of an independent audit of my Treasury unit, and secondly, to communicate my reform proposals on the financial software and the computer system.

With just days to go, there was still no official communication on who would be travelling to Luxembourg. So when auditor Barco, who had replaced Sachet, rang to agree a list of matters to be discussed at the meeting, I had to tell him, "I am still not sure whether I am going to be allowed to go – or even what the reasons are behind all this."

Barco appeared extremely concerned and said that he would alert others at the Court. But then – the day before departure – I received a note on the transport arrangements from which I assumed that I would be going. I wondered just how much more petty and childish this could all get.

Those making the two-hour mini-coach trip to Luxembourg eventually included, as well as myself, Maison, his deputy Mogen, and two other members of staff in charge of systems and inter-institutional relations. The visit started with a short meeting with the President of the Court of Auditors, Juan Manuel Fabra Valles – a man who was still recovering from serious illness – two other auditors, Victor Manuel da Silva Caldeira and Maire Geoghegan-Quinn, and with Maison, his deputy and myself.

Bluntly, Maison was asked if there was going to be any improvement in the 2001 accounts. He said he didn't know, "But I am sure they are not going to be worse than the year before." He added that as the Court of Auditors had always declared the accounts "reliable," if they were not better or worse, he was sure that the Court would not be able to change that opinion.

Clearly riled, Miss Geoghegan-Quinn pointed out that the court was not going to be inhibited from giving a very negative opinion, or even withhold an opinion, by that kind of argument. Also angered, Caldeira said he felt Maison's response – in the EU's bizarre vocabulary of near-English – amounted to "a form of harassment."

The President, Valles, now waded in in support of his two colleagues, stating that he was giving them full power to heavily qualify the accounts and even, if they believed it was necessary, to advise the European Parliament not to discharge them. Maison appeared surprisingly unruffled.

Following this meeting, there was a larger one where Maison was again heavily criticized for the lack of action in improving the accounts. He attempted to argue that this was the first time they had been able to get a qualified accountant as Chief Accountant. "It has been incredibly difficult to get people with the right background and qualifications for a lot of these vacant posts in accounting. Nobody applies."

At this point he was stopped by one of the auditors on the Court's staff, who exclaimed, "I cannot believe what I am hearing. I am a qualified accountant, with many years' experience of working in European institutions. I applied when Miss Andreasen was selected, and I was not even called for an initial interview."

In short, members of the Court clearly supported – or so I thought – what I was doing and suggested that Maison took account of the changes I was trying to bring about.

But back in Brussels nothing changed.

In my note to the Commissioner on the need for an independent Treasury audit, I had warned her that I was so concerned about the current state of affairs, and what it represented for the exercise of my signatory powers that if the situation didn't change I would feel obliged, as a professional accountant, to withhold my signature from certain documents such as payment notes, the authorization of bank accounts etc.

I got no response from Schreyer. But Maison called me into his office and demanded that I changed the terms of the note sent to her. He still refused to accept my request for an independent Treasury audit. He was highly critical of my proposal for expanding the use of the German computer software arguing that this was not my responsibility. I reminded him that it was.

I pointed out that while I was being pressured to produce my report on the accounting reforms, I had held back waiting for proposals from his computer systems team which seemed to be suffering quite inexplicable delays. "It makes absolutely no sense presenting accounting reforms which don't include changes to the computer system."

Maison warned me that he would never accept my proposals on the computer system. But then he qualified that it was of course the Directors General who were opposed to the German software, so I would get no support on that. This, however, sounded unlikely as they were the ones who claimed they couldn't manage their budgets on the existing system. We had been over this ground so often before.

Next, it was the turn of cabinet head Zimmer to ring and try to persuade me to rewrite my letter to the Commissioner – accepting full responsibility for the accounts, without reservations. He argued that I did not understand the real meaning of the financial regulations.

"I have read them and understand them perfectly well," I replied. I then tried to explain that the whole point of having a Chief Accountant was to have an independent and qualified voice to judge the probity of the accounts. "This is the duty I owe to the College of Commissioners, under the Treaties of Rome."

But Zimmer was either not listening or not understanding. He then suggested that if I did not agree with his interpretation of the rules then I should write to the Commissioner, relinquishing my responsibility. I pointed out that this was not what I was saying. Though unspoken, his attitude was clear: "Do what you are told or you are out."

I now realized that the time had come for me to face up to the fullest responsibilities of my job. The issue of possible computer changes had already been going on – round and round – for far too long. Maison was blocking my attempts to change a clearly vulnerable system. The Commissioner refused to respond to my warnings.

In the light of Maison's comment on the Directorates' reluctance to use the German software, I wrote to all the Directors General requesting their support for its implementation to help resolve the clear shortcomings of the current system. I pointed out that I had asked the Budget Commissioner for her authorization to implement these changes.

At 8pm on the night of April 22 – yes, I often worked that late – Schreyer summoned me to her office. She was furious, distraught, almost out of control about the letter and she accused me of trying to get her kicked out of her job or forcing her to resign. I could not believe what I was hearing.

Calmly, I explained about all the discussions within her Directorate, with the Court of Auditors and with herself about the computer systems – and Maison's dogged resistance not just to any significant change, but to any open, meaningful discussion of reform.

"The system I am proposing has already been designed and purchased by the Commission. We already have all the licences we need for its wider use." She had told me of her interest in developing it further. We had actually discussed it during my interviewing process. So what was the real issue here?

The real issue, presumably, was that Maison – finally exposed in a long-running saga of lies and obfuscation – had gone to Schreyer in a fury, and she now felt threatened because it was becoming obvious that although she had known about it for so long, she had done nothing to correct a clearly inadequate accounting system.

Schreyer threatened me with exposure of my suspension from the OECD. I told her that I had nothing to be ashamed of, quite the reverse, and that she was aware of this when she hired me.

At one point in the meeting, she actually broke down in tears as she reflected on the wretchedness of her position. I comforted her as best I could. "Things can't be that bad. If we can bring about change, you will be praised rather than censored. We should look on this as a great opportunity."

In fact, I was aghast, dumb-founded, appalled at her reaction to all this. I could almost have felt some sympathy for her – a clearly weak commissioner in the grip of an all-powerful, bullying bureaucracy – but I couldn't forget that the taxpayers of Europe deserved something so much better than what they were getting. This woman was earning some 200,000 euros a year, plus generous extras. Surely it was her job to stand up to pressure? After 20 minutes I slipped away.

The next morning, April 23, I was again called to Schreyer's office, where I found her accompanied by her cabinet head Zimmer and her spokesman. They began another onslaught on the letter sent to the Directors General asking me if I did not realize the impact on public opinion if such a letter were leaked.

I couldn't see that the public would be particularly interested in the technical details of a software programme. "Every year for the last six years, the Court of Auditors has been making public far more damaging revelations about the state of the EU's accounts. For anyone interested, there is nothing new here." Darkly, Schreyer's spokesman mentioned a certain German magazine journalist who was "always sniffing round for that kind of news."

A couple of years later I read in a newspaper that this same spokesman had made allegations against a German magazine journalist, Mr. Tillack (remember that name), which prompted OLAF to ask the Belgian police to raid the latter's office and take all his documents. Nothing was ever proved against Tillack and the European Court of Human Rights has recently granted him damages.

That same day, Commission Secretary General John Castle, who had never bothered to see me since my starting the job, also rang. But I was out of the office. It appeared that he had been very eager to see me before going into his weekly meeting with all the Directors General – where he expected reactions to my letter. I rang him back, now after his meeting, to find him still in a state of some agitation and we arranged to meet a week later on April 30.

Before then, I was called by cabinet head Zimmer to a meeting to discuss my responsibilities as Chief Accountant. I raised the issue of my independence as by this time the interventions of Maison had become flagrant and the Commissioner had not reacted to my notes. "As Chief Accountant I am responsible for the EU Treasury and accounts so it is clearly unacceptable for the Director General to decide the reform of the accounting system – and the staff needed for it."

At that point, Zimmer asked me to write a letter, transferring my responsibilities as Chief Accountant to the Director General. I refused – though at Zimmer's insistent demands I agreed to send him a draft expressing my reluctance to sign such a document.

Surprisingly, as soon as Zimmer received it his manner changed. On the phone, he said he entirely understood my concerns, that he would discuss the issues with the Commissioner and destroy my draft note. (Later, I found out that he had done no such thing.)

As the date drew near for the College of Commissioners to "adopt" the 2001 accounts, before sending them to the Court of Auditors, the Commissioner scheduled a meeting. When I arrived I saw that Maison had also invited my subordinate Villos – again without my being informed. But the one person absent who should have been there – to sign the accounts – was my predecessor Lematin.

The situation was absurd. Maison was now not only ignoring my responsibilities, my authority and independence – but he was also openly proclaiming that attitude to the Commissioner. I realized that I had been brought to the crossroads. Quickly, I had to decide what to do. Did I get up and leave? Did I stand up and tell the Commissioner that, as Chief Accountant, I was responsible for the accounts, and that, as Maison as Budget Director General was politically responsible for negotiating the annual budget with Parliament, his interventions could only be seen as representing a conflict of interest?

Or did I stay and say what I thought about the accounts? I stayed. Maison intimated that the accounts were now greatly improved – and Villos supported him. Wearily, I repeated the concerns that I had expressed in my earlier meetings with Schreyer. I explained that the last-minute reconciliation exercise had dealt with only the most glaring errors, and I indicated those areas where the accounts were still obviously unreliable.

As ever, there was little reaction. Maison told Schreyer that he would discuss his annual declaration with her privately. When the meeting – lasting barely 20 minutes – ended, Schreyer asked me to stay behind.

Immediately, both she and Maison demanded that I wrote a letter accepting full responsibility for the accounting and Treasury transactions, without any of the reservations I had spelled out in my previous correspondence with her.

Once again, I explained the problems and consequences of my doing that. The response from both was that I did not understand the financial regulations. I tried to explain – but they were not listening. Schreyer then threatened me by saying that she would ask the Director General to remove me from my job if I did not write the letter.

Later, Maison called me to his office to tell me that what

Schreyer wanted was a letter simply saying that I was sorry for having written to the Directors General to seek their support in implementing the German software system. I told him that I had not understood this.

But at that point, I felt that I had been caught in a trap. Either I signed some document they wanted – or I would have to go. I felt I had been treated appallingly – totally betrayed. I simply couldn't understand Schreyer's attitude. She knew what was going on and had hired me to sort it out. But why was she allowing Maison, who was responsible for the mess for the past 13 years, to block my proposals?

The only answer could be that she had become afraid for her own political future if she rocked the boat. She knew what Maison was like long before I did. She must have known that he could be quite unscrupulous when defending his own power base. She must have known that he would block any reforms and that, for me to succeed in such circumstances, I would need her support.

This whole long drawn-out nonsense about the computer systems could only have come about because Maison simply did not want an accounting system that was efficient and transparent – where people could actually see what was going on.

From a professional point of view, I knew that it would go against all of my principles to sign the sort of declaration that I suspected they wanted. If I did, I would then have to sign anything else they put in front of me. I would never be able to express any criticism or reservations on anything ever again.

These people knew that things were wrong – and wanted me to accept the responsibility for them. I felt like I was dealing with the Mafia. One crime – one hit – one indiscretion made by me on their behalf, and I would be theirs for life.

The only person I could think of consulting was Jules Muis – the Internal Audit Director General. But I found even him less chipper than usual. He was clearly concerned on my behalf – but, blocked in his own attempts at reform, he was struggling with serious issues that, I was to find out later, he couldn't yet talk about.

Focussing on my problems, Muis called in his deputy, and together they helped me work out a form of words, and the tone I should adopt, in expressing the extent, and limitations, of my job for a letter I later sent to Schreyer.

In his turn, Maison wrote to all the Directors General asking them to consider the letter that I had written, seeking their support, void. My options were closing.

Soon after that I had an experience that very much increased my worries. Living in a flat just half a mile from the Breydel 2 building, I often walked through a well-known park – the 'Cinquantenaire' – in the 'European' sector of the city.

One evening, as it was getting dark, I suddenly realized that I was being followed. I accidentally glanced back to see a man walking closely behind me. There was another one in front looking back at me. Quickly, I sat down on the nearest bench. The two men also stopped their walk, and waited.

I was scared and called my husband in Spain. He told me to calm down. "They are only trying to intimidate you. But you should get out of the park straight away." This I did immediately – and never went through that park again. But from that date onwards, I was often followed when I left the office.

I felt worried because I really didn't know what these people were up to. Were they just trying to frighten me? I couldn't understand their motives – but suspected there had to be a lot more at stake for an institution to organize such intimidation. I had read of how when the British official

Bernard Connolly was having his problems with the Commission, five years earlier, his house in Brussels had often been staked out by watchers at night when he was away. He assumed that this was an attempt to terrify his wife.

The Dutch 'whistleblower' Paul van Buitenen had also written of people lurking round outside his home – presumably to unnerve him and his family. How far were these people prepared to go? How dirty could this game get?

This form of intimidation was not only nasty but clever. How easy it must be to dismiss allegations ".. of being followed .." as the ".. ravings of a hysterical woman."

In fact, in this case it was easy enough to work out who was orchestrating this nastiness. On more than one occasion, I would get my husband, in Barcelona, to ring – and then, in Spanish, and in a voice slightly louder than usual, I would pretend to arrange to meet him at a nearby café in, say, 15 minutes' time.

Moments later I would notice that my secretary, also Spanish, would slip away from her desk, and occasionally I would follow to see her scampering up the stairs on some errand. Sure enough, 15 minutes later, when I left the building there would be someone loitering in the ground-floor lobby – ready to follow me to my spurious meeting.

But what were they trying to do? Find out if I were talking to the press – or simply trying to make me feel uneasy? They were already doing that on my computer. When I logged on, I could see that some files had been read at a time when I could not have been in the office. Sometimes, I clicked onto a file to find that it had already been opened – and was actually in use.

There were also strange new sounds on the phone in my Brussels flat. To test my suspicions, I went to a shop specializing in bugging-detection equipment to rent some simple device. "If your phone is being bugged, this green light will come on," the sales assistant explained. "Unfortunately, it won't be able to tell you who is doing the bugging."

Back in my flat, I made several calls – and after several seconds delay the green light flashed on. I was being bugged. But could the equipment be faulty? Down in the flat of the building's obliging concierge, I made several more calls. No green light.

Meanwhile, back in the office, Maison continued to organize meetings to which he invited my subordinates – but not myself. Since my staff kept me informed, I often turned up as well. It was while I was at one of these meetings that I got a summons from cabinet head Zimmer.

He wanted me to change the latest letter that I had sent to Schreyer after consulting with Muis. He threatened me with dismissal – but I left the office without signing the letter that he had demanded. I couldn't believe that they would think that I would accept full responsibility for a system that everybody knew was so widely open to abuse.

Indeed, I couldn't understand how they could so misjudge my personality as to believe that, by applying all this pressure, they could get what they wanted. How did they imagine that I would then be able to live with myself?

I had no doubt that Maison would do almost anything to eliminate me from his area of influence – and that he had got Commissioner Schreyer to fall in with his plans. What I couldn't understand was how she had been bent quite so easily to his will.

But then, in an organization run as erratically as the European Commission, maybe she had at some point put her name to something that Maison was able to intimate didn't put her in a fearfully good light. Wasn't this pretty much what they had been trying to do to me over the past few weeks?

With Maison and Schreyer so clearly opposed to reform, I now felt that the least I could do, as Chief Accountant, was to alert others in the institution as to just how badly the accounting system was failing – and the apparent efforts being made to obscure that fact.

I had hoped that my meeting with Commission Secretary General John Castle – scheduled for April 30 – might bring some support. But fairly soon after I entered his office, in the Breydel 1 building, I realized that he was another high-up determined to keep a quiet life.

He didn't routinely meet with recruits at my level, he explained as I sat down, but recognizing my responsibility as Chief Accountant he now conceded that in my case he should probably have done so.

With well-oiled charm, he then set off on a gentle ramble about the Commission's difficulties in dealing with so many cultures and – a respectful glance across his desk here – issues possibly to do with nationality and gender. He glided on to touch on instances of ".. people who have not always been treated well in the past."

In an effort to bring him back to planet earth, I told him bluntly that the situation that I was going through related very specifically to the lack of control of EU funds – for which I had to bear responsibility. "This is what I feel you need to be worried about and where I would appreciate your help."

There was a slightly pained smile, as he fell back on a mantra that I was to hear so often at the Commission. "No one is saying that we do not have some problems, but I feel sure that over time they can be fixed."

As I did not share his optimism, I decided to seek an interview with Commission President Romano Prodi – but then ran into the usual brick wall of bureaucracy. Clearly, direct interviews were out of the question. But while an assistant to Prodi's cabinet head assured me that my concerns would be passed on to the President, I was now well aware of the power that Commission officials had in filtering what their bosses were actually told.

Next, I sought an interview with the Briton, Neil Kinnock. Clearly, he was a key player as Vice-President of the Commission – and one of the four Commissioners to have survived the 1999 purge of the Santer Commission. As Commissioner for Internal Audit, Administration and Personnel, he had been appointed as the loudly-trumpeted 'reformer' to clear up the Commission's manifold problems.

Indeed, on appointment, he had explicitly promised to show zero tolerance for anyone in the EU who was indulging in fraud. The Commission, Kinnock declaimed, would be "effectively and transparently managed" and would give "value for money." The Commission itself was to become so squeaky clean, that it would actually emerge as a model of governance for other national governments round Europe and that ".. Eurosceptics would have nothing to complain about." Great stuff!

Kinnock had even allegedly set up a special charter for whistleblowers. But was I technically a whistle-blower – or someone just trying to do her job?

From Kinnock's office I again heard that no interview was possible. But in a meeting with his cabinet head, Jan Hoop*, he voiced his enormous concern and stated that my claims would be certainly investigated. They would get to work on that straight away. But I soon realized that absolutely nothing was going to be done.

On May 7, I contacted Hoop to tell him that I wasn't satisfied with the fact that I was asking for an interview with Kinnock and that this wasn't being granted. "I am now going to put my concerns to the Commissioner in writing." This cheered up Hoop in absolutely no way at all. But that same day I wrote also to the Commission's other Vice-President, Miss Loyola de Palacio, and to President Prodi.

I had been in the job for over four months now and had still not received any reply to any of the notes written to Budget Commissioner Schreyer. The only response to those letters had been pressure behind closed doors to get me to sign a letter – accepting responsibilities without limitations – on threat of dismissal.

It was only then, in early May, that I received a letter from Schreyer – in which she finally acknowledged ".. all the notes you have been sending." But rather than addressing any of the issues raised, she waded in, along with some personal abuse, with allegations that my staff had been complaining about me and that I had disrupted the service. Not content with this, Schreyer again summoned me to her office and repeated her demand that I sign a letter accepting responsibility for accounts for which I had not yet seen proper documentation.

I pointed out that I had already written her three letters on this issue and saw no need to write more. "I will sign for what I believe to be right – but not what I know is wrong or about which there are serious doubts." Once more, Schreyer threatened me with dismissal.

Meanwhile, my predecessor Lematin, who had been keeping his head down in Italy and resisting all invitations to complete a proper transfer of his old job to me, had also decided to weigh into the dispute. He wrote criticizing me for the letter that I had sent to the Directors General and accusing me of being ".. dismissive of the efforts of the Accounting team."

At first, I was surprised at seeing him getting involved in this particular smear. But then, with his former close colleagues having failed to bounce me into signing off the 2001 accounts, I could see that he was now part of a team effort which was changing tack. Their new charge was the allegation

– virtually impossible either to prove or disprove – that I did not get on with, or appreciate, my staff.

In my reply to him, I simply reminded him that he had not yet carried out a proper handover and not answered any of the specific points put to him in my letter of two months earlier.

Without too much hope, but on the advice of a colleague, I now asked for an interview with Gunther Gress*, Director General of Personnel and Administration. I had not met him since he had been part of an interview panel the previous September 11, and I had heard him described as ".. a man who will do what he is told to keep his career on track."

Indeed, my meeting with him, on May 13, only helped to confirm the Commission's essentially bankrupt philosophy and total disregard for justice, truth or equity. Gress chose to inform me that in any fight between a Commissioner and an official it is always the official who would lose.

Back in the Breydel 2 building, Maison's tricks were getting even dirtier. He scheduled a meeting to finalise the accounting reforms – without including any proposals on the computer systems – which would be sent to Schreyer, with whom we were convened to meet the following day. But just 20 minutes before the meeting it was cancelled.

That night I got a note from Schreyer informing me that I had failed to accomplish my duties as I had not yet sent her a draft of the communication on reform. Immediately, I responded that I had got the communication ready, but was supposed to get Maison's approval – as she had instructed – in the meeting that had been cancelled that same morning.

Maison then informed me that he had cancelled that meeting because I had not submitted my draft of the communication to him the night before. I responded that he had not made it clear that he had actually wanted it the night before – and that he had in any case seen an earlier draft, with the successive modifications made in response to his observations, insofar as they could be incorporated within a sound financial framework.

As our meeting with Schreyer to discuss all this had not been cancelled, I turned up at her office at the designated time – to be met by an apoplectic Zimmer who advanced on me angrily announcing that the meeting had been cancelled because of my failure to produce my draft communication on time. I tried to explain the reality and complexity of what had actually happened. But Zimmer was not to be deprived of his tantrum and he strode off with spectacular ill grace.

Eerily, I could now see them carefully setting up – with all the necessary histrionics – one ambush after another, in which they desperately sought to nail me with some specific dereliction of duty.

A few days later I got a call from Maire Geoghegan-Quinn's– whom I had met at the Court of Auditors on April 18 – cabinet head to let me know that copies of my letters to President Prodi and Vice-President Kinnock had come into their hands. "Did you mean to send them to us?" I said that that had not been my intention.

He said he would tell Fabra Valles, President of the Court, that I would write to them that that had not been my intention and that I was ".. not requesting help from them." I could only respond that, while I had not specifically intended that the letters come their way, I had no reason to write refusing their help.

I was puzzled by all this. In the past, the Auditors had so often shown themselves to be on my side. Several times, they had explicitly expressed the hope that I would finally fix the problems with the EU budget. There had been the support they had shown to me on my visit to them on April 18 – and the mauling they had administered to Maison.

Though I wrote to them – officially seeking their help – I wondered whether they were in fact seeking a way of "washing their hands" of me. I reflected that the Court of Auditors was not in fact truly independent – but also in the employ of the European Union. As well as its qualified professionals, it also, like the Commission itself, had its quota of political appointees. Had they also now been nobbled to line up against me and block any real reforms?

CHAPTER V

MY RESPONSIBILITY AS CHIEF ACCOUNTANT IS REMOVED

The following day, May 22, I was informed of a meeting to be held with Kinnock the next day – but without any indication of what it would be about. However, at 11am, an hour before the meeting was scheduled to take place, a letter was hand-delivered from Schreyer informing me that she was prepared to relieve me of my responsibility as Chief Accountant.

I wrote back immediately that it had never been my intention to be relieved of my job – and that I had always carried out my duties with professional propriety.

With the meeting postponed by some 40 minutes, it was 12.40pm when I was finally called to Schreyer's office. There, I found Neil Kinnock, Schreyer, Zimmer and Hoop already assembled around the meeting table. Kinnock, a 60-year-old Welshman, with his red hair now turning grey, was obviously in command of the show – and from the start his tone was bullying.

"There has clearly been a breakdown in the relationship with your Commissioner, Michaele Schreyer," he declared. The trouble was with Maison, not Schreyer, I pointed out. "The

Budget Director General has caused my relationship with the Budget Commissioner to become tense. The breakdown was not with her." Schreyer simply shook her head at this – but said nothing.

Kinnock ploughed on that they were planning to move me to another job in Financial Control. I pointed out that that made no sense. "In that new job, I will still be reporting to the same Commissioner. If you are saying that the problem is a breakdown in relationship with Miss Schreyer, then that problem is not going to go away."

Clearly irritated by any form of logic, Kinnock now reddened and became more aggressive, and declared that they could move me wherever they wanted to – with or without my consent. Calmly, I asked, "So why have you called me to this meeting, if you can move me without my consent?"

In fact, the reason now seemed pretty obvious. They wanted to remove me from the post of Chief Accountant where I had the authority and independence to argue for credible reforms – and also to tell other Commissioners, the European Parliament and Court of Auditors what was really going on with the accounting system.

Presumably, the meeting had been set up either to provoke or bully me into quitting my job and leaving the Commission in disgust – or to slink away with some cosy, quiet, well-rewarded deal. From the start of the meeting, Kinnock's whole manner can have been intended only to anger, intimidate or humiliate.

Unknown to me at that time, the day before this meeting Jules Muis had sent a private briefing note to Kinnock, his Commissioner, trying to warn him against any intemperate action against me. Flatteringly, Muis credited me with having ".. grasped the key issues at hand very fast indeed."

Kinnock should be ".. very wary of such a senior civil servant who was asking all the right questions." My reform proposals were "factually substantive and correct." Getting rid of me ".. would be a serious blow to reform, sending a signal that the old ways of keeping things from happening still work."

In fact, Muis's document – which became public only two years later – must have been one of the most scathing ever written on the Commission. In it, he described an ethos of poor spending controls and where I had struggled against an "intrinsically hostile work environment" beset by "a profound lack of qualified staff, a host of vacancies and absentees, an entrenched mindset."

He described the budget machinery as "vintage public sector in the 1960s" run by a French Director-General who "did not see the need for any accounting system at all." There was a culture of "arm-twisting," where "might makes right whatever one's professional convictions." The staff had a "top-down managerial mono-culture" and were in "a deep state of denial on the quality of the existing systems."

In a withering aside directed at Budget Commissioner Michaele Schreyer, Muis concluded that reform was doomed without a Commissioner "who has the stamina and spine to take a lot of shit."

For reasons that were to become only too obvious later on, Kinnock paid not the faintest regard to this document during our meeting – and indeed I suspect he even kept its existence secret from his fellow Commissioners in their deliberations on my case.

We concluded our ill-tempered meeting on that Thursday, May 23, with an agreement that I would have until the following Monday to ponder the proposed job change – and that no one would disclose what had been said to outside parties.

It was an agreement that had already been broken. As soon as I got back to my office I got a call from the assistant of an

MEP to say that Schreyer and Kinnock had been to the Parliament that morning – even before seeing me. They had spoken with members of the MEPs' Budgetary Control Committee – to tell them that they were preparing to dismiss me on the grounds of my ".. incompetence and dishonesty on recruitment."

Later that evening, I was still in my office when there was another call – long after my secretary had gone. Normally, I wouldn't have picked up the phone, but I thought it might be my husband Octavio ringing from Spain. "Could I speak with Miss Andreasen?" Wary now, I told the caller that she was not there.

"Well, I am a journalist with the German magazine Stern. My name is Hans Martin Tillack." (None other than the journalist already mentioned on page 60). "I would like to speak with Miss Andreasen to hear her opinion about her dismissal." Again, I pointed out that she was not there. "Where can I get hold of her? Because I have been told that the Budget Commissioner is right now writing her letter of dismissal."

I was staggered to have confirmation of my dismissal from a journalist. But that was by no means the only piece of underhand dealing. For example, Schreyer's letter informing me of the meeting that was to take place on May 23 had been dated May 22 – but it was only hand-delivered to me at about the last possible moment, at 11am, on May 23, just before my meeting with her. This was presumably to enable someone to falsely claim, at some later stage, that I had been given some form of adequate notice of what was happening.

The following day, May 24, Maison sent out a staff memo saying that on the Wednesday, May 22 – the day before I had seen Kinnock – the College of Commissioners had decided to relieve me of my responsibility as Chief Accountant.

Neither Schreyer, Kinnock nor anyone else at the meeting of May 23 had mentioned that such a decision had already been taken. On the internet, I saw that there was no reference to it in the minutes of the Commissioners' May 22 meeting. However the documents I obtained later in relation to my disciplinary procedure, confirm that the decision had indeed been taken on May 22 and before the meeting with Shreyer. By taking such precipitate action, they had seriously breached the staff regulations. These state that an official has a right to be heard before any decision is taken that may affect him or her. This initial and fundamental breach of procedure on their side was systematically ignored both by the internal disciplinary board and by the European Court of Justice. In his staff memo, Maison added that he had asked his deputy Mogen to take charge of the Budget Execution Director function – another decision on which the Commissioners had not yet made any public statement.

Of course, I was appalled at the callous and chaotic way in which this whole affair was being handled. My staff were now understandably concerned, making their way to my office to ask what was going on. Since Schreyer had taken it upon herself to inform MEPs of my dismissal before even telling me, I realized that the least I could do was to let them have my version of events.

To ten MEPs – representing a wide cross-section of different political and national groups – I registered my objections to being relieved of my Chief Accountant role and my surprise at hearing this justified by a personal fall-out between Schreyer and myself. Further, I detailed the real cause of the controversy: my concern over key failings in the management of Community funds.

Knowing that I had no witnesses on my side at the May 23 meeting with Kinnock and Schreyer, I sent my minutes of the discussion to all the Commissioners.

This enraged Kinnock's cabinet head, Hoop. Shortly afterwards he phoned in a rage to ask me why I had done that.

"Because you never issue minutes," I replied. "You were not taking any minutes at this meeting and I thought it right that people should have a true account of what was said." Indeed, when Hoop later released his minutes they differed substantially from mine – making no reference to the fact that I had stressed that the breakdown in relationships was essentially with Maison and not with Schreyer.

On boarding a flight to Barcelona that Friday night, May 24, two airport employees approached to deliver a fax from the Commission which I refused to take. It was clearly absurd that, with my having been in the office the entire working day, they should choose to deliver a communication to me through airport personnel.

The next morning, a friend in the UK rang to tell me that the Financial Times carried the story of my dismissal – which explained the Commission's desperation to deliver a fax to me at Brussels airport. The article itself could only have been written with a high-level briefing from people at the Commission.

Back in Brussels on Monday morning, Schreyer called me to her office to hand me a letter – dated Friday, May 24 – which informed me that, in its May 22 meeting, the Commissioners had decided to strip me of my job as Chief Accountant. She enclosed a page that seemed to be an annex to the minutes of the Commission meeting in which this was mentioned – (notwithstanding its earlier absence from the internet.) But the letter made no mention of the reasons for my dismissal, nor of my role as Budget Execution Director, nor where I would now be moved, nor any other decision about my future.

While I sat in my office, waiting for more news on this, Schreyer wrote to me – presumably in response to my May 24 letter to MEPs – alleging that I had accused Maison, herself, the entire Commission, Parliament, the Court of Auditors and Member States of promoting a new Financial Regulation that would simply increase the risks of error and fraud. She invited me to withdraw or substantiate such allegations.

She also said that she had always claimed in our meetings – when I had commented on the draft of the new Financial Regulation – that the regulation did not fall within my sphere of competence as Budget Execution Director.

In reply, I pointed out that, "My comments on the regulation were only on its draft – while it was still awaiting approval by Parliament and Council – and that it was my duty to alert people to its financial risks, as I have done on several occasions with you, the Budget Director General and his team." I offered to substantiate my concern over its financial risks – but this time in a public hearing before Parliament or the Council of Ministers.

Next came a letter from her – "answering on behalf of the President and Vice-Presidents of the Commission" – in response to my letters, written almost a month earlier, where I sought their support in implementing reforms.

Basically, she claimed that my observations had revealed nothing new and that it was in this context that the Commission had appointed me Chief Accountant: to prepare a draft communication on the modernization of the accounting system – which had to be cleared by Maison. She regretted that I had failed to do this – and intended to use this as the reason for my dismissal.

But in this letter, Schreyer rather shot herself in the foot. By claiming that the draft communication had to be cleared by Maison, she was essentially denying the independence of Chief Accountant. Indeed, in its various arguments to the public, and even later to the European Court of Justice, the Commission had always claimed that the communication of the accounting reform, and the reform itself, had to be the responsibility of the Budget Execution Director.

It was not until a week later that I heard from Kinnock that – in the "interest of the service" – I was being transferred from being Budget Execution Director to becoming a Principal Adviser at the Administration and Personnel Directorate. The Brussels equivalent of Siberia.

As that letter was being delivered, one of Maison's staff arrived at my office to pick up all the documents on my meeting table that were still waiting for my signature – but for which I had never received answers to my queries. No list of authorised signatories had yet been given to me either.

That same day I was moved to an office in the language centre building. It was small, with an inside view of a building well shaft, and had no other furniture than a cupboard, a desk and one chair. There was no telephone or computer connection, and my mobile phone was able to pick up no signal.

Soon after, I met with the Personnel Director General Gress to discuss the new responsibilities he was "thinking" of giving to me as a Principal Adviser. He referred to certain administrative aspects relating to the Research Centre at ISPRA – but without going into details. He said he would get back to me within the month.

In that time, Lematin finally got round to sending me papers that he chose to describe as a 'handover' document. "Here are the accounts for the year 2001," he wrote, "which you have to sign in approval." What was he trying to do: get my signature in receipt, and then claim this as some form of agreement with the accounts? As he had not signed them himself, from an accountancy point of view, they were completely worthless as a transfer of responsibility.

I still believed in the European Parliament, and that it should be told about the real reasons for my dismissal, and the seriousness of the Commission's lack of financial controls. So I introduced a petition to the relevant Parliamentary committee (Petitions Committee) asking to be heard by Parliament before the new Financial Regulation had been approved.

On June 20, I received confirmation that the petition had been declared admissible and that a letter had been sent to the chairwoman of the Budgetary Control Committee, in the European Parliament, asking them to hear me on my complaints about the accounting system and the Financial Regulation which had not yet been approved by themselves and the Council of Ministers.

Further, I also wrote to all the Spanish MEPs conveying my concerns and offering to explain them in greater detail in person.

After the report of my 'axing' in the Financial Times, the press started taking an interest in what was going on and how I was being treated. I refused to talk to them.

For their part, the Commission, obviously aware of the interest generated by their own abrupt and inexplicable firing of the Chief Accountant, continued to speak to the press freely – saying pretty much whatever suited them.

In a letter to European Voice, Kinnock's press spokesman baldly asserted that ".. Andreasen did not discover any new problems .." and in a bizarre travesty of the truth he claimed, "the Commission launched a reform of its accounting systems in 1999 .." reform that has ".. received approval from the Court of Auditors and has been carefully scrutinized both by Parliament and Council." Amazing.

Over the next few weeks, Commission officials variously briefed journalists that I had been fired because I was incompetent, couldn't get on with my staff; that my recruitment had been a mistake; that Schreyer had hired me only because she wanted another woman in the job.

Rather than recognizing that it might be fair to let me give my version of what had actually happened, Personnel Director

General Gress, wrote saying that it had been brought to his attention that I intended to meet with journalists – which was not the case. Stuffily, he reminded me of my duty of discretion "to preserve the relationship of trust which must exist between the institution and its officials."

Given the continued press briefing and whispering campaign against me by Commission officials, this sounded like a bad joke. I wrote back to Gress – citing Article 24 of staff regulations – asking for protection from the defamatory acts and utterances being made by Commission press officials and Budget Commissioner Schreyer. It was four months before he replied to this letter. By that time I had already been suspended for 2 months and Commission officials had spoken out publicly as much as they could against me.

At the language centre, my office remained bare and cheerless. Though the telephone was now working, I didn't trust using it. I had no job and nothing to do and few people to talk to. I found out that the building was being used pretty much as a repository – a penalty box or limbo – for others whom the Commission wanted to sideline or who had allegedly disgraced themselves in some way.

On July 2, I found a letter about me on the internet to Kinnock from the head of the Commission's legal service. Kinnock had apparently been seeking their advice on how to prevent me from appearing before the Parliament's Budgetary Control Committee in relation to the petition that I had introduced.

The head of the legal service advised against trying to prevent me speaking to Parliament by launching a disciplinary procedure against me. Indeed, he expressed doubt about the suitability, on legal grounds, of any disciplinary process being attempted, given that the issue ".. does not relate to concerns about actual wrongdoing, only to an internal difference of opinion, in this case about how to prevent possible fraud in future."

That very same day, Kinnock wrote telling me that a disciplinary procedure had been launched against me – and that I would be contacted for a hearing. He stated that the charges against me would be based on violations of staff regulations – in contacting the Court of Auditors and the European Parliament – and a failure to produce a communication on the accounting reform.

I didn't believe that any disciplinary procedure could progress on such absurd grounds. I felt encouraged that the Commission's own legal service appeared to share that view. It didn't seem possible that any court would uphold the claim that the Chief Accountant should not have the freedom to approach the Court of Auditors or even European Parliament – which is after all the body that has to approve the way that the Commission has managed taxpayers' money.

Jacques Mon – the person acting as temporary Chief Accountant after my removal – now asked that I sign the accounts for the period when I was in office: January to May 2002. This seemed like another bad joke as I had still not received a proper hand-over statement from my predecessor.

I wrote to both Mon and Schreyer that I would sign when I had been shown all the accounting records and books on which the financial statements were based. Needless to say, I never signed for my time in office. The records were never sent and indeed even such basic documentation was not kept by the Commission.

Advised by friends in the Commission, I now decided to take my case to the European Court of First Instance. This is the court that has the task of ensuring that the law is observed in the interpretation and application of the Community Treaties – and I appealed to it in December 2002, against my removal as Chief Accountant, and, in June 2003, against my suspension.

I looked for lawyers but, in the EU-dominated world of Brussels, found none willing to take my case on. So I decided to launch my own internal complaint against my transfer to the Personnel and Administration directorate as Principal Adviser.

This was the step I had to take if the court were to consider my appeal admissible. The Commission then had up to three months to respond, and if they did not, the complaint was deemed to be rejected by them and could then proceed to court.

On July 22, three weeks after Kinnock wrote to me about the opening of disciplinary proceedings, he wrote again: this time announcing his intention to suspend me. He told me that I would be hearing from the same official, Colin Wall, whom he had already appointed to investigate the earlier allegations – but from whom I had not yet heard.

For me, this threat of suspension seemed like the apogee of hypocrisy. I am not by nature a person who likes publicity, but as the Commission's press campaign continued against me, and I had had no response to my request for help on that from Gress, and was now facing the threat of suspension, I finally decided to speak to the press.

An invitation had come from Britain's Conservative MEPs to speak at a press conference in Westminster, and on August 1, 2002, I was at last able to explain publicly that the EU's accounting system was "massively open to fraud" as nearly all its transactions were impossible to trace.

"Even more serious, I was asked blatantly to contradict financial regulations by signing off accounts, despite knowing them to be untrue. I was not granted the freedom to address these shortcomings and, worse, actively discouraged from alerting others.

"Despite official press briefings against me and appearances on this issue by Commissioner Kinnock and his staff, I have been repeatedly reminded of my obligation to remain silent.

Commissioner Kinnock has even tried to prevent me from appearing before key parliamentary committees on these issues."

At that point, I decided to go on the holiday which I had applied for over a month earlier – and to which I had heard no objection. But as I was leaving on the afternoon of August 2, two officials approached me with a letter – which I indicated that I would accept on my return.

When I got back, I found correspondence that indicated that I had been called for a hearing on my suspension on August 7 – when officials knew that I would be away. There was also documentation on the delivery of a document, by notary, to a temporary concierge at my home in Barcelona – though this never reached my hands.

This all seemed to be part of the same harassing procedures that I had already seen on display when, having been in my office all day on May 24, the Commission had decided to wait, till the last possible moment, to deliver a fax by way of airport officials at Brussels airport.

On the day of my return from holiday I also heard from Colin Wall – the hearing official on the disciplinary procedures launched against me – calling me for a meeting on my suspension for the following day. I replied that I had no lawyer, and had not yet been given any of the details of the allegations made against me. I also notified Kinnock that, given the circumstances, I could hardly be expected to appear for any hearing.

Kinnock simply wrote back with more accusations: that I had been absent from Brussels on August 1 – the day of the London press conference – without permission, and that I had spoken to the press.

The next day I received a letter from the Commission that it had decided to suspend me. There was also a letter from the

Personnel Director General Gress outlining my rights and obligations as a suspended official. I would continue to receive my full salary, but was forbidden from entering any Commission buildings; I would have to continue living in Brussels and be available at any time.

But while Kinnock now seemed determined to pursue me with every minuscule, pettifogging, hair-splitting infraction of the rules on which he could scrape up evidence, it had recently emerged that his own behavior had apparently been less than squeaky clean.

Taking advantage of an arrangement whereby Commission officials were able to have their salaries adjusted according to the cost of living of their own country, he had been able to add another 20% to his annual pay. This concession had originally been intended for those who had to work in Brussels but, with young families or other problems, had to maintain dependents in their home countries, and thus might suffer unfairly by coming under the Belgian regime.

For a man whose two grown-up children had already left home, and had no need to maintain any dependents in the UK, the concession seemed unnecessary. Indeed, for someone already enjoying a free, chauffeur-driven car, an entertainment allowance of £7,000 a year, a £24,000-a-year housekeeping allowance, and whose MEP wife – on £55,000 a year and up to £115,000 in expenses – was in any case living with him in Brussels, this extra perk seemed, even to Commission officials, a teensy bit greedy.

Questioned on the BBC about this undeclared windfall offering – courtesy of European taxpayers – Kinnock simply snarled that it was "an entirely personal matter" and refused further discussion. In fact, he argued his entitlement to the concession with the Court of Auditors for a further two years before they finally saw things his way. Of course, they were paid out or the European budget which was managed by the Commission of which he was vice-president.

But for some, this hardly made him seem the whiter-than-white 'reformer' that they were looking for to reform and lead the great European project. They saw him more as a nitpicking martinet who was such a stickler for the rules as they applied to the behavior of other people, but not to himself.

Indeed, with talk in the air of my dismissal, and with some in the Commission apparently hell-bent on ending my career in Brussels, it was difficult to avoid the impression that there was some ambivalence in the application of EU rules.

So I was intrigued to read in the London Times, in September 2002, that over the previous five years the Commission had sacked just one person, although it refused to say for what. Yet the list of almost 50 cases of proven misconduct which might have persuaded most employers to part company with their employees included rape, fraud, forgery, assault, harassment, misuse of funds, theft, and possession of paedophile pornography. In the majority of cases, the offenders were given reprimands, written warnings or "admonitions." A total of 15 were moved to other posts or demoted.

With this relaxed, laid-back attitude towards their own employees' errant behaviour, it seemed odd that some Commission officials were still going to such lengths to prevent a former Chief Accountant speaking to the Community's own parliamentarians about what was happening to their taxpayers' money. But the fight over my petition to address the Parliament's Budgetary Control Committee rumbled on, with its MEP members finally agreeing that I could do so - subject to the approval of the Conference of Presidents.

This was composed of the heads of the Parliament's various political groupings. But a month later, in October 2002, they announced that they could not allow such a hearing as I was ".. under disciplinary procedure .." and the ".. inter-institutional agreement signed does not allow them to hear a disciplined official." This wasn't actually true as, at that point, the disciplinary procedure hadn't started, and was deemed only as "possible."

Presumably, someone in the Commission had helpfully provided them with a way out of hearing me – which had been seized on with alacrity. Of all the various Parliamentary groups only the EDD – the European Democracy and Diversity Group – had been willing to hear me, but they had been well outnumbered by the giant battalions of MEPs representing liberals, socialists, conservatives, neo-fascists and others.

As mentioned earlier, this was the same Parliament that year after year – notwithstanding the Court of Auditors' reservations – gave discharge to the Commission's annual accounts. But maybe this simply represented the rules of what Maison in his immortal words described as the 'inter-institutional game' between Commission and Parliament: 'you let me do what I want and I'll let you do what you want.'

A handful of MEPs were enormously helpful, energetic and supportive on my behalf, but too many represented a poor return on their salaries of some 80,000 euros a year and a pathetic attitude towards their constituents' enlightenment, wallets and the whole issue of free speech and open criticism within the European Union.

Before the year was out, however, I had finally located – after a four months' search – a lawyer, prepared to represent me in my case against the Commission, and to work on a pro bono basis. He was a man who appeared to be on my side.

CHAPTER VI

SUSPENDED FOR 18 MONTHS AND MY DISCIPLINARY PROCEDURE

The disciplinary process unrolled against me continued at glacial pace and with scant regard for natural justice. The whole notion of suspension was that it should be an 'interim measure' to cover some emergency situation that had to be dealt with quickly.

In my case, I did not get to see the official appointed to investigate the allegations – Colin Wall*, Director General of the EU's Publications Office – for nearly four months from the date of Commissioner Kinnock's letter, of July 22 2002, threatening me with suspension.

In the almost surrealistic, looking-glass world of the EU, I then heard from the Dutch 'whistleblower' Paul van Buitenen that Wall was himself under investigation, as his department was named in a hefty 234-page dossier – backed up by 5,000 documents – that van Buitenen had passed on to OLAF.

Van Buitenen – not yet elected as an MEP, and describing himself simply as an EU citizen – nevertheless took it upon himself to fire off a letter to Commissioner Kinnock, protesting various features of the case thus far: the fact that Kinnock had initiated disciplinary procedures against me – despite the advice of the Commission's Legal Service and Investigation and Disciplinary Office not to do so.

He pointed out that Kinnock had nominated the Director General of the EU Publications Office, as president of an inquiry into me, despite the fact that his department was itself under investigation by OLAF.

While Colin Wall had recently written to me, calling me for a hearing with a view to a "possible launch of a disciplinary procedure," Kinnock had communicated to the European Parliament that I was already under disciplinary procedure. This meant that the conference of presidents, at the European Parliament, voted by a majority not to hear me in their Budgetary Control Committee.

Despite the fact that Wall had interviewed other officials about my case, he had refused to supply either me or my lawyer with copies of the relevant 'invitation letters' or minutes of the hearings – claiming secrecy.

This was in direct contravention to assurances made by Kinnock to van Buitenen in 2001, when Kinnock had asserted that an official under inquiry had the right to such information for as long as the case was open.

In the event, OLAF never came up with anything on Wall that they felt warranted prosecution, and after van Buitenen's letter had received the usual dyspeptic brush-off from Kinnock, the first hearing finally took place in Luxembourg, where the EU Publications Office is located, on November 19, 2002. I was accompanied by my lawyer.

Wall, a 57-year-old man, gave the impression of making a genuine and meticulous effort to elucidate how I had been recruited and treated during my time with the Commission, as some half dozen of us sat round a table in his office.

He didn't mention, however, that he was already in the process of interviewing 15 witnesses – all of them Commission employees and understandably, with regard to their careers and pensions, unlikely to rush to the cause of a person they could see being crucified. More to the point, he didn't invite me to nominate any witnesses of my own.

At one point in the hearing, Wall raised the sexist issue – he muttered that it must have been difficult for me to be surrounded and up against so many men. Yet I had never seen the problem as a sexist issue and I had no intention of letting the investigation be diverted into that muddy backwater.

Although minutes of this meeting, and Wall's witness interviews, were completed before the end of 2002, I was not able to get hold of a copy of his full report until April 2004.

During that time I was honoured with the Frode Jacobsen Award – for civic honesty and courage – in Denmark, and voted Personality of the Year by the readers of Accountancy Age magazine in Britain.

While waiting to hear from the Commission, I was invited to speak at professional conferences on matters related to internal controls, risk assessment and strategies to combat fraud among other things. As I didn't receive any fees for these talks, and as my presentation related to the importance of having a reliable accounting system as the first step to preventing fraud, I saw no reason for declining such invitations.

I made it clear that I spoke as the former Chief Accountant of the European Commission and mentioned only those matters already in the public domain – such as the Court of Auditors' reports, Commission Accounts or the post-Santer report of the 'Wise Men.'

It was only in September 2003, when Personnel Director General Gunther Gress wrote to me, that I became aware that, even as a suspended official, I needed permission to give such talks. In writing back, I assured him that everything I spoke on had already been made public and I duly asked for permission for those talks that I had not yet given. According to my reading of staff regulations, I knew that such authorization could not be denied ".. unless the activity is contrary to the interests of any EU institution."

It was clear that not even the EU could withhold permission without recognizing that the interests of the EU were not the ones they proclaimed and that the lack of controls was in their real interest.

Gress duly granted permission. Yet two months later, in November 2003, Commissioner Kinnock – back in Archangel Gabriel mode – wrote informing me that as I had spoken at earlier conferences without permission there would have to be another hearing into this.

It was difficult to avoid the suspicion, however, that this latest flurry of activity on a matter of such mind-numbing triviality was partly an effort on the Commission's part to show that they had maintained some contact with me during those long months when absolutely nothing was being done on the disciplinary process. Further, the objection which Kinnock now raised about my earlier unauthorized conference talks could be interpreted as a somewhat desperate attempt to add to a dossier of thus far very feeble complaints against me.

The hearing into the matter was held in Brussels, on February 19, 2004, and consisted of Colin Wall working his way through the press coverage of the meetings and conferences to which I had been invited in different parts of Europe. Had I spoken about this aspect of the Commission's work? Had I mentioned that?

Eventually, I told Wall that I was unwilling to answer any more of his questions. "If you have any specific allegations to make against me, I will answer them. I can only repeat that everything I said about the work and accounting of the

Commission was already in the public domain. If you have any evidence that I spoke otherwise, let's see it."

The following month, March 2004, I finally heard from Personnel Director General Gress that a report had been sent by the Appointing Authority to the Disciplinary Board – an action that represented the formal start of disciplinary proceedings against me.

But it was to be another month, April 7, before I finally got hold of Wall's report. From the date stamp on its cover, it was evident that it had been received by Kinnock's office on April 23, 2003, and had thus been sitting there for almost a whole year. Yet, when my lawyer had inquired, at my behest, about its progress the previous July (2003) Kinnock's staff flatly denied having yet received it.

It was also fairly obvious that there had in fact been two versions of the report. As well as having two separate cover sheets, there were so many instances where its fairly harsh conclusions – "serious infringement of Staff Regulations" – simply didn't fit with the facts that Wall had so meticulously recorded.

Could it have been that the first report concluded that there was no case for dismissal, and then the hapless Wall had been informed that he had somehow missed the whole point of the exercise – and that he had better to get back to work?

Some of the witness statements included in the report gave a wildly skewed version of events. Maybe the memory of Pierre Sachet, of the Court of Auditors, was playing tricks with him when he asserted that it was I who insisted on a meeting with him in January 2002 – (having been in the job for one week, if you please) – and that it was I who had launched a verbal assault on Maison and his colleagues and their working methods. An exact reversal of the truth.

In fact, I had spent all of one hour, at just one meeting with Sachet. Why were there no witness statements from others at the Court of Auditors, with whom I had worked in frequent and productive harmony over several months?

As if this documentation was not bad enough, the composition of the Disciplinary Board itself was alarming. Only its President, a Portuguese judge, who had retired from the European Court of First Instance, could be seen as having some mildly independent status.

All four others – senior civil servants of or above my grade – were still serving members of the Commission. Since all four were current, and apparently satisfied, participants in a clearly vulnerable accounting system, they were hardly likely to come down on my side.

Under staff rules, I could have rejected all who had been proposed. Discussing this with my lawyer, he argued that if I behaved well, and showed myself to be amenable, I was likely to receive ".. a very light sanction .." from the board. But there was one proposed board member – under investigation himself, and allegedly up to his neck in trouble at Eurostat – that I insisted had to go.

As well as Wall's report, the board now dumped on me and my lawyer all the paperwork relating to the case – a file amounting to some thousand pages. They then announced – having refused us sight of any documents at all for the previous 16 months – that the first meeting of the board would be held in two weeks' time: April 21, 2004.

I urged my lawyer not to accept this date as we would clearly need more time to read and analyse all that we had been given. But he was as sanguine as ever. He had been assured by the President of the Board that the first meeting was simply an 'organisational' one at which we would agree an agenda for the future hearings.

Essentially, the charges against me were that I had not gone through the proper protocol in lodging my complaints about the accounting system – (despite the fact that Maison had not only attempted to block any reform but any discussion of reform); that I had not gone through the correct hierarchy in voicing my criticism to the Court of Auditors – (despite the fact that the Court had approached me directly, making almost similar complaints from the start of my time in office as Chief Accountant); that I should not have aired my views to Parliament – (despite the fact that Kinnock and Schreyer had told MEPs of my planned dismissal, before informing me); that I should not have spoken to the press without permission – (despite the fact that Commission officials had spent the entire summer of 2002 briefing against me); that I had not told the Commission of my suspension from the OECD – (despite the fact that Commissioner Schreyer had herself raised the issue in our very first telephone conversation); that I had spoken at conferences without permission – (relating information that had in fact already long been in the public domain).

It was difficult not to compare the strength of these charges against me with the latitude extended to the wilful and freewheeling ways of Monsieur Maison during the time we had been together in office. For over a period of five months, the Director General had comprehensively ignored Treaty rules on my independence as Chief Accountant, and on my overall authority over computer systems. He had put all kinds of pressure on me to sign accounts for which there was no proper documentation. He had done nothing to insist on a proper handover process from my predecessor on my coming into office; he had repeatedly failed to provide a comprehensive job description of my appointments; and he had often allowed temporary officials to sit in on highly confidential Commission deliberations.

All in all, I felt the case against me was so weak that it was something that any vigorous advocate should have been able to blow out of the water at the first hearing.

In the event, the first hearing, at the Directorate of External Relations, on April 21, was both nightmare and disaster. My lawyer, who was in any case involved in another big case at the time, took it upon himself to start rewriting his introductory statement for the court on the morning of the hearing itself.

Five minutes before we should have left his office, he was still making changes that I did not get the chance to see. At one point in this shambles, I discovered that he proposed telling the court that I apologized and was prepared even to be downgraded. I was not.

Eventually, we arrived at the court ten minutes late. Not a good start. There were some eight of us sitting round a large table. As soon as he opened the proceedings, Martin Berry, the senior member of the Board, and Director General for External Relations – demolished any notion that I was to get a fair hearing. We had arrived late, and he informed us that he had little time to waste on such matters. In other words, we should say what we had to say so that he could be off.

My lawyer summarized my case – my attempts to rectify an accounting system that was badly failing the taxpayers of Europe. To this Berry replied that this was a political world and those who did not agree with the policies of their superiors should resign. He then stalked out.

From there, things only got worse. For the next 20 minutes, the four remaining board members – and with no judicial or any other kind of formal procedure – bombarded me with questions on statements I was alleged to have made, culled from the European press from over the previous two years. All were extremely hostile and aggressive about what one saw as my "disgusting behavior."

And that was it.

As neither my lawyer nor I had been supplied with any of the documentation of this latest catalogue of complaints, it was clearly a lost cause.

When the board set a date for the next hearing – for just two weeks later – I pleaded with my lawyer to ask for a postponement. I knew that we needed far more time. The whole thing had become absurd; all this rush and mess when the Commission had taken nearly two years to launch proceedings.

Bluntly, I had to tell him, "I am not ready for this second hearing and I don't believe you are either." We had a row about it. Unfazed, he simply told me that he had spoken with the secretary of the Board, who had told him that its members were actually on my side. Given their conduct, proceedings, views and manners at the first hearing, I found this hard to believe. But then I could see no other pro bono lawyer on the horizon, and I could not afford a proper one.

At my lawyer's insistence, we went ahead with the hearing scheduled for May 7, at which Commission lawyer, Luc Sanden*, did his best to downplay the responsibility, independence and powers of the Commission's Chief Accountant. In fact, the EU Treaties and staff rules were quite clear that the Chief Accountant had both pecuniary and legal responsibility for the accounts being correct. I badly needed a lawyer who could pick his way through the legal thicket of rules on these points and present the essentials of my case with clarity and vigour. Sadly, that lawyer was not on display on May 7.

My dissatisfaction with my lawyer came to an abrupt head a few weeks later when he failed to pass on my requests for documentation to the Board. Obviously, it would have been legally risky to suggest that he had been out to sabotage my case from the start. Well knowing the ways of the Commission by then – and its amazing medley of tricks for 'getting at' people – I was appalled.

So I decided to fight the case on my own. At that point, given that I had not been allowed into any Commission building, or had had access to their records for almost two years, I asked for various documents crucial to my case – including the annual declarations of the Directors General. I also requested the minutes of the Disciplinary Board's meetings on my case. These were refused and only part of the other documentation arrived – a month after it had been requested.

By then the Board had at least conceded the right for me to nominate my own witnesses – given that the rules laid down that ".. if the sanction to be imposed is believed to be more serious than a warning .." then the person facing disciplinary action could bring witnesses.

A hearing of these witnesses was initially set for before the summer break. But as some of the officials involved had requested holidays for that period, the Board scheduled the hearing for September 9, 2004. This was a date on which they had already been informed that neither I, for pressing family reasons, nor one of my three witnesses would be able to attend. I remonstrated with them – the hearing went ahead anyway without us.

One of my witnesses did, however, submit a statement for this hearing. This was the gallant and forthright Jules Muis, former Director General of Internal Audit, who had lasted at the Commission only until April 2004 – just three years into his post. I then found out some of the pressures that he too had been under at the Commission, and that he couldn't talk about, when my own troubles were reaching crisis point.

Indeed, Muis went public in citing very much the same difficulties as myself, in cutting down on fraud and waste, and in his inability to conduct sweeping audit inquiries. "I look forward to the Commission (defining) what it wants with the Internal Audit Service (IAS), because that is not clear even to me."

He pointed out that the Commission's financial report, which he read on taking office had been "shockingly primitive." Since then, an improvement had been only "gradual." He reckoned he had achieved only "40 per cent of what I wanted to do, and all of it has been uphill."

He was to go into even more forceful detail on some of these points in the eloquently blunt statement he made on my behalf for the hearing on September 9, 2004. In it, he asserted that he knew of no professional accountant having to start their job with as vulnerable and undefined an opening balance sheet as I had.

"I would for no money or professional reward wanted to have been in Ms Andreasen's professional shoes when this all played out, recognizing the unforgiving inclination of a bureaucracy, once one is declared taboo by the powers that be .. and .. considering the collective firepower it can marshal to trash an individual it has singled out."

He suggested the Commission take heed of the signals the case would send out to other accounting professionals, if it were resolved on the basis of power politics alone.

Generously, Muis conceded that his own Internal Audit job seemed, by comparison, like a picnic given that he had no immediate ".. money flow/disbursement operating responsibilities." Also, he did have Director General status, though ".. This did not stop one Chef de Cabinet from telling me once in private, 'We have ways of breaking people like you.'"

He insisted that I was very much the outsider in a sink or swim situation in a very unfriendly pond – and in a directorate with "an incestuous esprit de corps ... not particularly taken by aliens imposed from a different world."

Though he felt that the accounting and auditing of the Commission and Court of Auditors showed ".. a major long-standing compliance gap with standard practice," he believed that of the five different Accountants he dealt with in his first two years at the Commission, "Miss Andreasen is the one and only who … focused professionally .. on the integrity of the Commission's accounts; and expected to be held accountable and liable if proven wrong."

"With all the control mishaps of the Commission, I do not recall any Commission Accountant (other than Miss Andreasen) stepping up to the plate saying, 'I am the first accountable; what are your questions?' – or being held accountable for close to ten years' gross, substandard financial reporting."

He suggested that this could explain the attitude problem of the Budget Directorate throughout those years, and why the other four Chief Accountants, in contrast to myself, took the traditional bureaucratic line of process responsibility only. "One even said to me that he '.. does not sign the accounts; he only sends the accounts.'"

That meant that ten years after the Commission first failed to get normal audit approval on its accounts and controls, it still didn't have a proper accountability system, and that the Budget Directorate still only accepted ".. (open-ended) process responsibility, with no end product responsibility, hence the incentive to get it really right is not there." For Muis, this did much to explain the wretched position in which the Commission now found itself.

But not even this powerful, detailed, considered, well-informed critique appeared to do much to take up the time or impact on the deliberations of the Disciplinary Board. The very next day it issued its decision: dismissal.

Did it bother members of the Board that the two most senior officials on the accounting and auditing side of the Commission – Muis and myself – had gone within the space of two years, and both making very much the same criticisms? Apparently not.

The Disciplinary Board's 14-page report did, however, reveal the real essence – the real motivation – the real poison – of the case against me. This emerged in its slippery accusations of lack of loyalty and discretion.

On the one hand, the Board proclaimed that, "All Commission officials enjoy the right of freedom of expression" .. (even here) ".. it extends to opinions which dissent from or conflict with those held by the employing institution."

On the other, the Board's report contended that the freedom of expression ".. should be exercised by officials with due respect to the principles of loyalty and discretion laid down in Articles 11 and 12 .. of Staff Regulations ... The official must not act in a way which jeopardizes the relationship of trust with the institution concerned."

In other words, in simple language that people, at least in the Anglo-Saxon world, can understand, the European Commission doesn't really believe in the freedom of expression at all. Whatever care I had taken in trying to register my concern, whatever bureaucratic hoops and procedures I had gone through, they would always have been able to argue that, in their interpretation of clearly conflicting laws, I had breached " the laws of loyalty and discretion" owed to my superiors.

In fact, over several months, my superiors were urging me to sign off accounts which, unsupported by proper documentation, would have constituted not simply an illegal but a criminal act. Yet somehow my refusal to do so was showing disloyalty to these people, and my protests at such attempted coercion had been "detrimental to the honour of the persons" applying this pressure.

This sounded to me like the double-speak of the old Soviet nomenklatura. Catch 22 and the 'Newspeak' of George Orwell's 1984 both also came to my mind.

This pretty well confirmed not simply the hopelessness of my case, but the near-impossibility of anyone effecting real change within an undemocratic and essentially lawless institution: the European Union.

The whole process following my removal and suspension – but particularly the Disciplinary Board proceedings – appeared to me to be a travesty of natural justice. But what struck me most of all was the arrogance with which they didn't even bother to go through the motions of pretending to provide a fair trial.

The staff regulations provided for an official in my position to be heard by the Appointing Authority before the final decision was taken. In my case this meant that it had to be a hearing in front of the whole College of Commissioners. I was eventually granted this meeting on September 29, 2004 – 20 days after the Disciplinary Board had issued its statement.

Having gone through all the previous stages of the disciplinary process, without anyone appearing to make the least effort to engage with the issues I was trying to raise, I wondered whether this meeting with the Commissioners would be another meaningless charade.

Yet I was still determined to face them and make one more attempt to impress upon them the negligence with which so much of their taxpayers' money was being handled and to reiterate, again, urgent solutions.

For this meeting I had got a friend, Chris Dickson, who was the executive counsel of the UK Accountants' Joint Disciplinary Scheme, and who had massively wide professional experience, to make a statement on my behalf. At his own expense, he had flown over to Brussels the night before, to make sure that he was there for the 9am start of the hearing.

But before the proceedings in the Breydel 1 building got under way, Commission lawyer Luc Sanden directed Dickson and myself into an anteroom next to the room where the hearing would be held. There he attempted to get us to sign a confidentiality note, binding us to secrecy on the proceedings.

Dickson was outraged that such a request should even have been made without a similar commitment being sought from the Commissioners. Further, he pointed out that he had no intention of being inhibited from saying whatever he thought fit in my defence, either to the public or in any later court hearing.

Knowing that Commissioners and Commission officials had felt free to say whatever they wanted about me since my departure from office, I had no intention of signing any note of confidentiality either.

After that, we moved into the rather cramped hearing room, taking our places at one end of a long oblong table, round which sat 21 of the 24 Commissioners. At the far end, Michaele Schreyer, sitting between two other female Commissioners, struck a pose that might have been seen as warm and supportive – but came across to me as simply cowed and uncomfortable.

Also at our end, on our left, was Commission President Romano Prodi. Several places away on our right, sat Kinnock, whose behavior appeared to have regressed to that of a schoolboy. He made exaggerated and dismissive gestures with his arms, as if to register his disgust at what I was saying and alert his colleagues that the lady in front of them was completely mad.

Other Commissioners occupied themselves with reports or paperwork that were clearly nothing at all to do with the matter in hand. Some, who had not bothered to turn off their mobile phones, would occasionally, when rung, wander off to have telephone conversations in the corridor outside. Only the Italian Competition Commissioner Mario Monti appeared to take an interest in what was being said.

None even seemed particularly interested when Dickson was invited to speak and informed them that he believed that I had brought to the job the professional qualities that all good accountants have. "The first of these, and the most important, is that of independence, both of thought and of action."

He explained that as one who spent much of his time looking at corporate disasters involving accountants, particularly those who audited financial statements, he found that the single biggest contributing factor was the auditor who was not prepared to stand up to his or her corporate client.

"Too often defalcation has gone unpunished because of willful blindness, whilst considerable thought, and chargeable time, has been expended in devising means for corporate clients to circumvent accounting standards."

He believed that the second crucial quality that I had displayed had been the instinct to question – not just how the organization in which I worked actually functioned, but the financial implications of what was being done, and their controls.

"You would be surprised by how many bad accountants I come across who either have not made the effort, or who have not had the intellectual capacity, to understand the business in which they are working, or which they are auditing. This problem has been seen not only in sophisticated sectors such as those involving complex financial instruments, but also in the public sector where, in many western countries, governments have sought to move expenditure off their own balance sheets and onto those of the private sector. The critical analysis by an accountant of what is actually happening is crucial."

The third quality that he felt I had shown was that of responsibility for what I did, and an understanding that genuine assurance could come only through having separate responsibilities for different people. He instanced such key procedures as having a small number of authorised cheque signatories; two signatures on each cheque; no person to sign a cheque which benefits him or her; insistence on original documentation rather than photocopies or faxes; and asking someone independent to review and audit the financial information.

Dickson betrayed his amazement at the way I had been treated, when he remarked that, "Judging by some of the papers I've seen, one might be forgiven for thinking Miss Andreasen was being accused of fraud rather than trying to prevent it."

But not even Dickson's lucid statement – like the testimony of Muis – appeared to have the slightest effect on those gathered there. As the proceedings concluded, Commission President Prodi asked if anyone had any questions. To this, the answer was a sepulchral silence.

It was clear that the decision had already been taken and that most who had come there had done so mainly to register their lack of interest, boredom or contempt. For a group of people, ostensibly in charge of 100 billion euros of EU taxpayers' money per annum, it was not an edifying performance.

In about a month – November 2004 – virtually all those Commissioners there would be leaving at the end of their five-year term, to make way for a new Commission. But before gliding off for a well-rewarded retirement, they did manage to squeeze in one more act of monumental discourtesy.

On October 13, 2004, I was driving through Barcelona, when my mobile rang. It was a journalist asking for my comment on the decision to dismiss me from my job at the Commission – which had just been announced. I had to tell him that I was not aware of this decision.

Back home, I found an e-mail that had been sent to me 15 minutes earlier, informing me of the Commission's decision.

But obviously, no one had made any real effort to make sure that I knew before my dismissal was made public. Pretty much the same as day one.

As well as the studied contempt they had shown for me throughout the proceedings, I was staggered by their complacency. For while this group of highly-paid public servants was poring over such hair-splitting issues as to whom, as Chief Accountant, I should or should not have been able to speak, or whether I had got permission to speak at some conference, huge sums were still leaching away from the EU's coffers.

Just the year before, 2003, the Court of Auditors had estimated that 50 per cent of suckling cows which were claimed to be grazing in Portugal did not exist. Eighty-nine per cent of farms in Luxembourg had submitted claims for payments based on an inaccurate acreage which, if believed, would have swollen the country way beyond its tiny borders.

In Greece, one enterprising farmer, who claimed to have lost 501 sheep to wolves between 2002 and 2004, continued to claim subsidies for the 470 sheep he had started off with – and without producing any evidence of restocking.

Even more expensive was the chicanery that had been going on at Eurostat – the EU's statistical branch. In September 2003, after four separate investigations had been grinding on for some six years, this finally emerged into daylight.

A preliminary report exposed what it described as a "vast enterprise of looting," including cases of fictitious accounts and controls, inflation of contract prices, slush funds, double accounting and serious breaches of the rules governing tenders. Taxpayers' money had ostensibly been used to pay for perks and freebies, including a riding club, a volleyball team, extravagant dinners, and trips to New York and the Bahamas.

When the scandal first broke I regarded it almost as "help

from heaven" as it illustrated so graphically and comprehensively so many of the warnings that I had been attempting to give since my arrival in office as Chief Accountant. For the bottom line was that no real investigation into Eurostat could be completed because the audit trail – all the documentation – either didn't exist or had by now disappeared. Further, the whole sordid business emphasized the dangers of not knowing exactly who had signatory authority on bank accounts.

Would these revelations at last stun the Commission into a realization of the inadequacy of its controls and the depths of its problems? Not a bit of it. When a special task force and internal auditors produced interim reports in September 2003, the Commission did its utmost to keep their findings under wraps.

The reports were certainly not to be published. In a shabby deal between the Commission and European Parliament – citing "legal" reasons – they were to be shown to only a select group of MEPs. They were given just five hours to peruse them in a sealed room, under the surveillance of security guards, and without any access to photocopiers. They were banned from taking in mobile phones, cameras, or notepads and had to sign a declaration promising not to reveal the contents of the reports.

When Commission President Prodi held a "hearing" on the reports' findings in the European Parliament, it was in camera, and with the leaders of the Parliament's political groups – not with the more "awkward" MEP members of the Budgetary Control Committee.

Many believed that this collusion between Pat Cox, the President of the European Parliament, and the Commission, to hide the full facts from public scrutiny, to be in itself a separate scandal. As the London Times put it, "If the Commission has nothing to hide, its secretiveness is incomprehensible. If it has, it is inexcusable. Signor Prodi has muzzled the European Parliament; he must not be allowed to hide the truth."

But this was an affair with so many separate scandals. As the possible dimensions of the losses became clearer, Pedro Solbes, the Spanish Commissioner for Economic and Monetary Affairs, was invited to resign but refused. He claimed to have had no knowledge of Eurostat problems until he read about them in the press in May 2003. Yet his own office had requested a report on one particularly controversial contract almost a year earlier.

Solbes finally moved on only when a vacancy became available for him as Minister of Economy in the new socialist government of Jose Luis Rodriguez Zapatero, which was elected in March 2004.

Eurostat's Director General and two other senior officials - who were closely connected with some of the outside firms gaining Eurostat contracts, and at the very least should have known what was going on – were discreetly transferred to other jobs or allowed to slip away into full-pension-rights retirement. Not one of them had to face any form of disciplinary action.

Indeed, the only people who appeared to have suffered in this sorry affair were those who had been attempting to expose what was going on. Dorte Schmidt-Brown, a Danish economist who had joined Eurostat in 1993, did her job properly and in 1999 alerted her managers to contracts which seemed highly suspicious. One, she felt, had been awarded unfairly to a company run by a former Commission employee, which had never carried out much of the work for which it had been paid highly-inflated fees.

An internal audit inquiry later supported her allegations. But she was first of all ignored, and then sidelined in her job. In an interview with the Brussels-based weekly European Voice, in October 2003, she revealed that she had suffered a nervous breakdown after her disclosures. Eventually, after going on a very long sick leave, she secured an invalidity pension from the Commission.

Few people made more efforts to expose the rottenness of Eurostat than the German journalist Hans-Martin Tillack. He was the one who had rung me on the night of May 23, 2002, to inform me that Commissioner Schreyer was at that moment writing my letter of dismissal. Presumably, he must have had good contacts with someone close to Schreyer's office to know that.

But even the luck of this hard-digging, well-connected journalist was to run out. At 6am on March 19, 2004, he was woken by six Belgian policemen, who came into his flat, held him prisoner for ten hours and then, after ransacking his home and office, confiscated two computers, four mobile telephones and 16 boxes of documents, archives, personal papers and bank statements. He thus lost the notes that he had carefully built up over five years. His sources were also put at risk.

Refusing him access to any lawyer for ten hours, police asked who his sources were. Tillack insisted that he would never reveal his sources. "The police told me I was lucky I wasn't in Burma or central Africa, where journalists get the real treatment."

It turned out that this raid had been done at the behest of OLAF, on the allegation that Tillack had paid for evidence used in articles exposing EU corruption in the German magazine Stern.

At a meeting in the European Parliament building shortly after he had been released from custody, Tillack was heckled by MEPs angry that he had given ".. ammunition to the anti-Europeans."

Ironically, Tillack never had been against the EU. Describing himself as a "pro-European Federalist," he was simply against corruption.

In an effort to prevent the Belgian police handing his papers over to OLAF, Tillack went to the European Court of First Instance. He was supported in this action by the International Federation of Journalists. The evidence against him had by then been clearly shown to have been fabricated.

But on October 15, 2004, the European Court of First Instance threw out his claim – even though that judgement was in clear breach of rulings by the European Court of Human Rights that a journalist has the right to protect his sources.

Tillack's lawyers had argued that the protection of such sources is a cornerstone of a free press, and of genuine democracy. But in vain. The ruling effectively gave the Commission the power to persecute any journalist who dared delve into the murkier corners of the European Union. For some it brought back uncomfortable memories of the sort of totalitarianism that had darkened Europe in the 1930's and 1940's.

It took Tillack another four years, until 2008, to get his papers back from the police – and it was only in November 2007 that he got some redress in the Courts. In a landmark decision, the European Court of Human Rights ruled that the Belgian police had violated his right to the freedom of expression and ordered the Belgian state to pay him 10,000 euros in moral damages and 30,000 euros in costs.

Ironically – and in one of those bizarre twists that possibly only the European Union could pull off – Tillack's award worked out at about the same as that given to two other European citizens in July, 2008, following a ruling by the European Court of First Instance. For the court ruled that when the law had eventually turned its gaze on Eurostat's former Director General and director, both OLAF and the Commission had broken procedural rules in an investigation that never came to court.

OLAF had concluded that both men had committed illegal irregularities regarding Eurostat financial procedures, and handed files to the Luxembourg and French judicial authorities.

The European Court of First Instance, however, ruled that OLAF had "infringed the rights of defence" of the two men by "referring to them publicly – including through leaks to the press – as guilty of criminal offences." This, said the court, breached mandatory principles of the presumption of innocence; the obligation of confidentiality in investigations; and the principle of sound administration. These "wrongful acts" entitled them to damages, from the EU, of 56,000 euros.

Wasn't that nice?

With the collapse of my case in front of the Disciplinary Board in late 2004 it was to the European Court of First Instance that I too was then headed.

CHAPTER VII

APPEALING TO THE EUROPEAN COURT OF FIRST INSTANCE

In November 2004, still without a lawyer, I launched an internal complaint against my dismissal as Chief Accountant. This was a prerequisite before taking a case to the European Court of First Instance. But as this was a procedure on which the Commission would be invited to give a reaction, they were usually able to drag the process out for another three months.

At about that same time, I received a letter that a hearing had finally been set for the cases of my transfer and suspension that I had originally introduced at the European Court of First Instance in December 2002 and June 2003 respectively.

I decided to ask the Court to withdraw both cases as the appeals had been overtaken by events – given that I had now been dismissed. I considered it useless pursuing them as, even if I got a positive decision on either of them, it wouldn't affect the decision to dismiss me that had already been taken by the European Commission.

But even withdrawing those two cases proved difficult. The European Court of First Instance wouldn't accept a letter from me but insisted that my former lawyer, make the request formally.

I asked him to write – but he prevaricated, then got his lawyer colleagues who had been involved in the case to try and talk me into continuing with the two cases.

In the end, he agreed to ask for a postponement of the hearing. This was not what I wanted, but for the moment it was my only way out of an absurd situation as by then he was refusing point blank to ask for my cases to be removed from the register. A lot of time was lost in this way – time that would have been far better spent in my trying to get myself a completely new lawyer who was enthusiastic about my cause and whom I could trust.

By this time the new Commission of Jose Manuel Barroso was in place and for some months in the autumn of 2004 I had some hope that they might review the decision to dismiss me and take a more favourable approach to reform of the Commission's accounting systems.

In press interviews, Barroso had spoken of his eagerness to sack any Commissioners suspected of poor or fraudulent behavior. "There is a need for political leadership, for political courage, and I will try to show that leadership."

He saw himself as a person who upheld the values of open societies. "So my most important influences are the liberal thinkers of Europe and America, such as de Tocqueville and Karl Popper." Great stuff!

Even better, he appointed Siim Kallas of Estonia as Commissioner for Administrative Affairs, Audit, and Anti-Fraud – the first time a commissioner's title had formally incorporated the word: Anti-Fraud.

My good and very supportive friend and Danish MEP Jens-Peter Bonde even arranged for me to have a private talk with Kallas. But the evening before the meeting should have taken place in early December 2004, it was cancelled. Kallas wrote to Bonde telling him that, on the advice of the Commission's legal service, he was to have no contact with me. Indeed, a few days later, Kallas announced that my plea for a stay of execution of my dismissal had been rejected by the new Commission.

But by then Barroso's credentials as the fearless opponent of wrongdoing were beginning to look a bit shaky. For in putting together his new Commission, he had proposed the appointment of the Frenchman Jacques Barrot, who in 2000 had been convicted of electoral fraud – after diverting £2 million of French government money to his political party, the Centre of Democratic Socialists. He had been given a suspended prison sentence of eight months.

When his good friend Jacques Chirac, President of France, granted Barrot an amnesty this meant that, technically, the conviction was expunged. Legally, it had never happened. And since the conviction never happened, the French press were forbidden even from reporting that it had never happened!

Barrot made no mention of it to Commission President Barroso, nor to MEPs. When the news eventually leaked out and MEPs discovered they were about to confirm as commissioner a convicted fraudster there was a Parliamentary storm. But Barroso continued to affirm his "100 per cent" support for his nominee. MEPs swallowed their objections and Barrot went on to become first, Commissioner for Transport, and a Vice-President of the Commission, and then in May 2008 he was appointed to his current post of – wait for it – Commissioner for Justice, Freedom and Security.

And these were pretty much the same people who had been working themselves into such a lather over whether my suspension from the OECD should or should not have been included on my CV – despite the fact that the OECD's independent auditors had supported me, despite the fact that I had mentioned it to Maison at our first meeting, despite the fact that Maison had consulted with at least three different people at the OECD before my recruitment, and despite the fact that Commissioner Michaele Schreyer had raised the issue in her first telephone conversation with me.

In my case, though the Commission had announced their decision to refuse my request for a stay of execution on my dismissal, this was not the complete answer to my claim as I still had an appeal outstanding with the European Court of First Instance, with regard to the dismissal decision itself.

But in the early months of 2005, I was still finding it difficult to find a lawyer who was prepared to take on the Commission in such a case, and to charge the sort of fees that I could afford.

In the end, I decided to apply for the Legal Aid which is provided by the European Court of Justice Regulation. They, however, sent my request for "comments" from the Commission who, being the defendant, refused my request point blank. In natural justice, the Commission should clearly have never been involved. But this was yet another classic example of the lack of judicial independence – of the essential separation of powers – with which the EU institutions work.

In fact, by that time the whole legal process had become even more weighted against those in dispute with the Commission. For not only had the Commission started sending its own lawyers to fight cases where before this had not been deemed necessary, but the plaintiff had become liable for the institution's legal expenses when losing a case. This was a penalty that did not exist before and which would allow only the richest or most foolhardy to bring an action in future.

In finding myself a lawyer, I had to deal with further residual problems posed by my relationship with my former lawyer. For while it is common practice for a lawyer to hand over all documentation to his successor if there is a change of counsel, he refused to do this. He would only allow copies to be made of certain documents in his office. It was difficult to see this other than a ploy to make it extremely difficult for another lawyer to take over the case.

Eventually, in May 2005, I found a young Belgian lawyer, Julien Leclere*, based in Luxembourg, who was willing to act for me. With him I began preparing an appeal, in French, which we finally presented on June 5, 2005.

On his advice, I concentrated on those aspects of the case that the European Court of First Instance were likely to declare admissible for judgment. These basically had to do with the legality of the procedure which led to my dismissal, and the violation of the European Union's own laws and staff regulations.

There were of course plenty of breaches that could be cited. I had a right to a fair trial – guaranteed by article 6 of the European Convention on Human Rights. Yet there had been a clear lack of independence of members of the Disciplinary Board – all of them Commission officials who had been managing EU funds without proper controls for years.

In addition, the College of Commissioners who took the final decision on my dismissal included Neil Kinnock and Michaele Schreyer who had been my original accusers – and thus judge and jury on the case.

Further, my powers and authority as Chief Accountant had been comprehensively ignored from the start of my time in office.

With regard to my alleged violation of staff regulations, Article 21 actually spelt out that while an official had a duty to help his superiors, if asked to do something against the law, he should raise the issue with his managers and, if still instructed to do so, should proceed only if that request were made in writing.

In fact, I had always discussed my concerns on legality with Budget Director General Maison and Commissioner Schreyer, and also put them in writing – but had never received any written response.

On the contrary, my letters had led only to closed-door meetings where I was subjected to verbal pressure to sign off accounts, and assume authority for transactions which were clearly against the rules, under threat of dismissal.

Another important aspect of my claim was the way in which the Commission had ignored a staff regulation – (Article 10(96) of Annex IX) – in considering the proportionality of my dismissal. For staff regulations state the sanction has to take into account the level of responsibility of the official concerned and the circumstances in which the alleged misbehavior had taken place.

It was clear, for example, that communicating with the Court of Auditors on matters related to EU accounting could not be judged as misbehaviour when performed by the Commission's Chief Accountant.

It was also clear that the negative annual reports from the European Court of Auditors were an expression of how bad things were and also of their level of concern about this. The letters they wrote to me after my recruitment simply confirmed that they were looking to me for urgent resolution of these problems.

The actual legal procedure was long and tedious, as once I introduced the claim, the European Court of First Instance sent it for a response to the Commission. Though they had two months in which to do so, they asked for an extension and ended up taking four.

What made it worse was that the Commission's response went way beyond what many would have considered reasonable in length and complexity – and would possibly serve only to tire and confuse the court. For while my original appeal consisted of 31 pages of legal arguments and 107 pages of annexes, they responded with 60 pages of legal arguments and 400 pages of annexes. Rather than attempting to restrain this legalistic overkill, the Court had simply granted them additional time.

In essence, the Commission insisted that the case had nothing to do with the concerns that I had raised about the accounting system, but related only to my "behaviour." They thus treated themselves to 27 pages of legal argument, in an interpretation of the letters that I had written to the senior Commissioners, that had little to do with the actual spirit of the law. Moreover, they insisted that I had no right to write to the Commissioners themselves – despite my role as Chief Accountant.

In the end, the two rounds of responses, and written procedure alone – with the extensions allowed to the Commission – spun the whole process out to March 2006.

By then it was too late for my case to proceed in the European Court of First Instance. For in December 2005 an entirely new body called the Civil Service Tribunal came into being. This had been created to deal with staff cases which had formerly been handled by the European Court of First Instance.

Given the amount of extra time allowed to the Commission to complete all their written procedures – and with their failure to meet a deadline of December 15, 2005 – my case was transferred to this new Civil Service Tribunal.

This meant that there was another massive delay and it was not until November 23, 2006, that we finally appeared before the Civil Service Tribunal – eight months after the written procedure had been completed, and a good two years after my dismissal had been announced by the Commissioners.

As we filed into court, in the modern Allegro building in Luxembourg, it was difficult not to note the contrast between their team and ours. They had two lawyers, who swished in, dressed in white cravats and black gowns, followed by two legal assistants; whereas on our side, we had just one lawyer, also in cravat and gown, but who hobbled in (his leg encased in plaster from a sports injury), my husband and me.

As we arranged ourselves at the three sets of desks, facing the three judges on their plinth, the Commission lawyers proceeded to pile up no fewer than six boxes of legal documents. We had just the one fairly slim file.

Apart from this grand entrance, there was nothing impressive about the ensuing legal proceedings. The presiding judge, a Belgian called Sean Van Raepenbusch, had worked for some part of the Commission's legal services since 1984; the reporting judge was a Finn, Heikki Kanninen, and the third judge was a Polish woman, Irena Boruta.

The proceedings were in French but as the three judges spoke so little it was difficult to know how well all three really comprehended the language.

The Finnish judge, Kanninen, asked most of the questions – starting with the application of the new and old staff rules. This clearly caused some unease among the Commission's lawyers as my lawyer, Julien Leclere, was able to show that they had applied them in a random, indiscriminate way that had best suited their case.

The key point in the hearing came when Kanninen asked about my responsibilities as Chief Accountant and my lawyer asked the tribunal if I could answer that question myself. At this point, the presiding judge, Van Raepenbusch, managed to change his expression from one of boredom to annoyance.

Kanninen asked the Commission lawyers if they had any objection to my speaking. Reluctantly, they agreed as long as I was not allowed to start telling my full story – a limitation to which Van Raepenbusch enthusiastically agreed. "Yes, Miss Andresen, (sic) please keep it short."

Briefly, I explained my responsibilities on the accounting and treasury aspects of the EU budget, which was worth more than 100 billion euros at that time. I also pointed out that while no job description had ever been given to me, the EU Treaties and Financial Regulation were quite explicit on the extent of my authority.

At this point, the Commission lawyers intervened to attempt to argue that the Treasury function at the Commission was of little significance. But this still seemed an extraordinary view, given that the Commission's main reason for existence was to pay out subsidies from the funds contributed by its Member States. I couldn't believe that the judges could possibly accept such a specious argument.

In fact, it was difficult to work out whether any of the points made during the 45-minute hearing had impacted on the judges in any way at all. The Polish woman judge opened her mouth only once: to ask why the disciplinary procedure had taken so long.

The Commission lawyers argued that this was because I ".. went on committing so many new offences" – (as if I were some naughty girl in a boarding school). But then I didn't really feel that the woman judge's question had been prompted by any particular warmth or sympathy on my behalf.

Indeed, before the hearing had even ended it was difficult to avoid the impression that the whole procedure was just another empty formality – a ritual that the Commission felt that it had to go through so that it could later claim to have provided some form of fair trial.

At its conclusion, I was given to understand that the Tribunal would announce their decision within the next six months – by April 2007 at the latest. In fact, it was almost a year later – on November 8, 2007 – that they finally handed down their judgement. In it, they dismissed all nine breaches of the Treaties and due process that I had presented against the Commission.

Indeed, it was a judgement that didn't appear to have had any recourse to case law and could have been virtually dictated by, and for the convenience of, the Commission. All the points made about the lack of independence of the Disciplinary Board members, and those Commissioners who had laid the allegations against me, were simply ignored.

Further, they appeared to disregard all documentary evidence – including that provided by the Commission's own lawyers – on my right, as Chief Accountant, to have direct contact with the Court of Auditors and European Parliament. For example, the advertisement for my job explicitly stated that its holder ".. will be also in charge of the contacts with the Court of Auditors (of the European Communities) within the framework of the (declaration of assurance) and the financial statements."

In other parts of the judgement, it appeared to rely solely on the opinion of the Disciplinary Board members who, as previously pointed out, were those who had been happy to manage funds on a system that was clearly vulnerable to abuse.

So after waiting more than five years after my departure from office for a verdict that would recognize that I had acted in line with my professional duty, I simply got a confirmation of the absolute contempt in which the Commission appeared to hold my responsibility as Chief Accountant.

All in all, it seemed almost unbelievable to me that the judges would find it admissible that the Chief Accountant of the

Commission should be sacked merely for stating clearly what the Court of Auditors had said every year for the previous 13 years. Indeed, within ten days of the Tribunal's judgement being made public, the Court of Auditors refused, yet again, to sign off the EU's accounts, complaining of "fraud, neglect and irregularities."

(Further, in September 2008, Commissioner Kallas, Kinnock's successor in charge of reform, admitted that he did not expect the Court of Auditors to give the Commission's accounts a clean bill of health until 2020!)

Clearly, I will not give up – and I still have the right to challenge the Civil Service Tribunal's judgement in the European Court of First Instance.

Before that judgement was made public in November 2007, my lawyer had already alerted me that if the case went against me, he would not be able to act for me in an appeal as he had been recruited to head up the legal department of a private company where that sort of work would not be possible.

He did, however, manage to find me a third lawyer, also based in Luxembourg, whom I travelled to see and brief extensively on my case. But the next day, after my return to Barcelona, there was an e-mail from the third lawyer informing me that he would not be able to represent me after all because of " .. a conflict of interest."

I managed to find out what this "conflict of interest" was all about. In one of those quite amazing coincidences that appear to govern so much of life in the European Union – in the less than 24 hours between my last conversation with the third lawyer, and my flying home to Spain, he had been offered a job by the Commission to train officials in its legal service. So there I was, back to square one.

The helpful Leclere did, however, manage to locate yet another lawyer: Benjamin Marthoz. As I had only two months in which to appeal the Civil Service Tribunal's judgement, I had to work flat out with him in early 2008 to register my appeal with the European Court of First Instance.

This was where I had started off almost three years earlier – before being diverted on to the Civil Service Tribunal – for a legal merry-go-round that might best be written up by Charles Dickens or Franz Kafka.

Why do I go on? Partly because I know of the discomfort of the Commission when every single one of its decisions is challenged in any hearing, court or tribunal and lets even the tiniest chink of daylight into a judicial process that is not independent – but simply part of the political development of the European Union.

Indeed, the main reason that I continue to fight is that I don't want my children – and possibly their children – to live in thrall to the EU: a layer of government that, in my view, is not only unnecessary, but lawless, corrupt, mistaken, undemocratic, bureaucratic, over-regulated and, ultimately, unworkable.

Even if the EU does not develop into a full, single political entity, what has happened so far is quite bad enough. Its parliament – without powers to propose legislation – is hardly in any real sense a Parliament. Its executive (the Commission) – headed by political appointees – is barely accountable to anyone, apart from the very blunt instrument of its entire dismissal by Parliament, as happened with the Santer Commission in 1999.

Is it possible for the EU to change, to reform? Having worked in it, and seen it from the inside, I see no chance of that. I see the institution as not only corrupt but corrupting. For it is not just the individual cases of money going to Madame Cresson's dentist, or for non-existent olive groves, that is so disturbing.

It is the whole lax, insulated, isolated culture in which officials work, knowing they can ignore the rules with impunity which should give thinking people cause for concern.

During my entire time at the Commission I met few who seemed concerned about this – and even fewer who felt they should exercise responsibility and try to change what was going on.

Possibly some expected that I too – as the beneficiary of a nice salary, nice office, nice allowances, nice perks, and with the prospects of a nice pension – would have played the EU game of endlessly passing responsibility onto someone else.

When the very few who do stand up and protest, or even quietly inform their managers of what is going on, are so consistently and so easily 'trashed,' can any European of sound mind actually believe in the possibility of reform?

The British MEP Daniel Hannan once eloquently lamented the state of affairs in which, "We are so blasé about Brussels fraud that we no longer notice it. It doesn't even make the newspapers any more: that's the shocking thing. While the auditors are happy to vouch for the money raised by the EU, they cannot say where it goes.

"What makes the EU behave like this? Its employees are not inherently wickeder than anyone else. All organisations have their share of shysters. The difference is that there is no link in Brussels between taxation, representation and expenditure. The EU expects bouquets when it spends, but not brickbats when it taxes, because its revenue is handed over by national treasuries.

"The truth is that EU fraud is, in the correct sense of the word, structural: a product of how the Brussels institutions are set up ... and I have (now) reached the view that the system is beyond reform. When (Eurocrats) disparage their critics, they confuse cause and effect. We are not banging on about corruption because we dislike the EU; we dislike the EU because we see it for what it is: a racket, whose chief function is to look after its own.

"Finally, let us deal with the assertion that, since much of the EU's spending is disbursed by national and regional authorities, Brussels ought not to be blamed for their failings. It is certainly true that the money trickles down through many levels, like champagne through a pyramid of crystal flutes.

"But this is the problem: in such a system, no one has an incentive to behave properly. The applicants, knowing the cash is there to be claimed, arrange their affairs so as to qualify for it. National authorities have no interest in policing the system, since it is all EU money. And Eurocrats are happy to sign the cheques in the belief that they are buying popularity."

Hannan went on to define what he sees as ".. the worst aspect of Euro-corruption. In my own constituency, I have seen how the people most directly ruled by EU law – fishermen – have been forced to alter their behaviour to comply with the Brussels way of doing things.

"I have seen honest men turned, against their will, into liars and cheats by the Common Fisheries Policy.

"The disease is not confined to Brussels: it is contaminating our own body politic, carried by cash handouts through our veins and arteries. After years of looking vainly for a cure, it is time to consider amputation."

Will this little book help to bring about early reform of the EU and its accounting practices? I fear not; turkeys do not vote for Christmas.

But I hope that it lays bare what really goes on in Brussels. I also hope that it will make more people aware of what really goes on behind the gloss and the tinsel and the avalanche of publications telling us how wonderful and indispensable the EU is. There are already those who believe that the whole thing will collapse from within, under its own incompetence and corruption. I do not share this view. Only if enough ordinary citizens in Europe become sufficiently angry with their Governments for going along with it all, might change come about.

Of course European nations should work together to meet such challenges as terrorism, border control, financial crises and climate change; but this can be done by intergovernmental collaboration between consenting democracies. Democracy is the guarantor of peace, not unaccountable bureaucracy.

Europeans do not need to go on surrendering their sovereignty, their integrity and their future to a corrupt and incompetent mega-state. When will they see this?

EPILOGUE

I have no doubt that the European Commission will dismiss my story by claiming that "it was all a long time ago", and that its accounting and control systems have since been made altogether wonderful. However, its failure to get a clean bill of health from the European Court of Auditors for the last 14 years is proof that nothing much has, in fact, changed and that the European Union remains an open till waiting to be robbed. The only real change since my dismissal is that the Commission has shifted the blame onto the Member States. That's where the billions go walkabout; it's entirely their fault now (which isn't true, of course).

In one thing they have succeeded. No employee has dared to 'blow the whistle' since they got rid of me. I suppose they have all seen what has happened to me and they know that I couldn't get another job at my professional level anywhere in Europe; no other employee has been prepared to irritate the beast in Brussels.

But I have not given up my fight. I did not give up a powerful and well paid job just to see this bureaucracy, the integrity of which I experienced from the inside, continue to roll over us. Back in 2002 I raised my concerns with Mrs. Diemut Theato, the Chairwoman of the Budgetary Control Committee of the European Parliament. In real life she was a translator. I had the incredible experience of trying to make Mrs. Theato understand what the problems were in the management of the EU's budget. She happily acknowledged to me that she had no knowledge of finance or accounting, and therefore couldn't understand what I was talking about. Imagine my frustration! How could this worthy lady, with her background, be in a position to challenge what the European Commission was telling us about its accounting and control systems? How could she exercise any influence over European taxpayers' money if she had not the faintest idea about the subject?

With this experience in mind I decided to stand in the South East Region of the UK as a UK Independence Party candidate for the European Parliament in the June 2009 elections, and am very grateful to have been elected. With this new responsibility I therefore propose to join the Budgetary Control Committee and challenge each and every one of the numbers in the EU accounts. In effect, my mission is now to go to Brussels and find out how the British people's money is being spent, and then come back to tell them the truth.

I know where the bodies are buried.

Marta Andreasen, MEP
July 2009

HOW IT CAME ABOUT THAT
ST EDWARD'S PRESS LTD PUBLISHED
MARTA ANDREASEN'S STORY
"BRUSSELS LAID BARE"

A NOTE BY H. M. WILLIAMS

I am the managing director of St Edward's Press; and I
believe it might be helpful if I explain how it has come
about that this very small publishing house finds itself
publishing what is unquestionably an important book.

Before I retired at the end of December 2014, my main
occupation was not, in fact, publishing at all, but
accountancy. For over forty years I was the senior
partner of the accounting firm that I founded. It was in
this capacity that I first became aware of the existence of
the newly-appointed EU's chief accountant, Marta
Andreasen, when her name started featuring in the Press
in 2002. To my horror, I learnt that she was being
punished for refusing to sign off the EU's 2001 accounts,
which had been prepared by her predecessor, and which
she could see contained a glaring error (in fact probably
not an error but a fraud) of €200 million.

Her initial punishment for refusing to gloss over this
matter was to be suspended. Her criticisms of the
accounts were then investigated for two years; they were

found to be fully justified but, instead of being rewarded and thanked for her integrity and courage, she was sacked. I was appalled at this injustice, both as an accountant (naturally) and also as a Christian. I could hardly believe my eyes as her brave fight for honesty and justice was being so ruthlessly trampled on by the EU.

Nonetheless I was working away in Plymouth and these events were taking place in far off Brussels, and there was little I could do about her plight – or so I thought at the time.

In 2003 the magazine, *Accountancy Age*, ran a poll amongst its readers to choose the "Accounting Personality of the Year". Every year this magazine runs an awards evening in London - a huge event attended by over 1,000 accountants and their guests. I am pleased to report that Marta won the award for that category in 2003, I being one of those who voted for her.

The following year, 2004, my business partner and I decided to enter our practice for an *Accountancy Age* award (for "Best Small UK Accountancy Firm"). We were nominated, which meant that we were in the top three; and we were therefore invited to attend the annual *Accountancy Age* jamboree. When leafing through the paperwork in advance of this event, I was intrigued to see that, as a past award winner, Marta was one of the judges. This really got me interested, to the extent that I said to my wife, Alice, that I would far rather meet Marta and shake her hand, than win a national award.

At the end of the awards ceremony (and, no, we didn't win the award) I advanced from the mêlée to where I thought I would find her, and, lo and behold, there she was sitting at the front all on her own. I introduced myself, and explained that our firm had been nominated for an award. Her first words to me were "Ah, Mr Williams, I recall your nomination and I would like you to know that, while you didn't win, _I_ voted for you." A good start as far as I was concerned!

After that brief meeting, we remained in email contact. A little later, an accounting friend of mine, Andrew Hamilton, who, at that time, ran his own practice in Edinburgh, wanted to put on a talk about EU accounting for his clients in 2006, and, knowing that I knew Marta's contact details, asked me if I would introduce him to her, which I gladly did. Andrew also invited me to this event, where I was privileged to give the vote of thanks at the end. In turn, this meeting led to a second similar one later that year. And one way and another, Marta and I gradually became firm friends and this led to my seeing her on quite a few occasions, during one of which I suggested to her, as indeed had others, that she ought to write her story of what happened while she was in Brussels.

She started writing in 2007 and in the spring of 2008 she gave me the manuscript to read. I was not disappointed - even in that early form, it was a devastating tale, a real jaw-dropper. But it was also clear that, that while Marta's English is excellent, her first language (of many) is Spanish, and that if the book was to have the appeal it deserved, we would need to get a professional wordsmith to do some work on the script. Marta and I agreed that I should hand the manuscript to Lord Pearson of Rannoch who knew of a retired journalist and the result, as you will have seen, was a really first-rate page-turner. The story now reads like the thriller it was in real life.

The next step was to find a publisher. In November 2008 one was duly found, and Marta was told by him that copies of the book would be ready in February 2009. But the thriller that is Marta's EU story had further to go! In February 2009 I duly telephoned her to ask if the book was ready, only to be told by a crest-fallen author that the publishers had decided not to proceed with the book after all. Thus it came about that I now stepped forward and offered to publish her story, but not without hesitation on my part. St Edward's Press was, and still is, a very small publisher, with, at that stage, just two publications to its name. And although it certainly knew how to produce a book, it could not claim any significant marketing power or expertise, and on the face of it was therefore not an ideal option for Marta. But mine was the only offer open to her and she very graciously accepted it.

The book was finally launched on 11 May 2009, at a party at St Stephen's Club in Westminster. I owe a huge debt to Lord Pearson who hosted that party and also to many others who helped me get this important book into print, but who, for reasons that readers of the book will easily understand, have asked me not to mention by name

As to Marta herself, well, to find that I, an obscure accountant from the depths of Devon (where I then lived), have published this devastating story for *the* most famous accountant in the world, and one who is also an exceptionally brave and diligently honest woman, is a privilege beyond my wildest imaginings. Thank you, Marta, for entrusting this important work to me.

I hope that it is in order to close by saying that, from reading the reviews that have been given to this book on Amazon, I like to think that her story has played a not-insignificant part in achieving the result that the UK voters gave in June 2016, when asked the question, "Should the United Kingdom remain a member of the European Union or leave the European union?"

Hugh Williams
Managing Director, St Edward's Press Ltd.
info@stedwardspress.co.uk
Autumn 2009 (Updated May 2017)

FORM FOR ORDERING MORE COPIES OF THIS BOOK

How to order

If you would like more copies of this book please complete, tear out and send this form in one of the following ways:

- **Post to** St. Edwards Press, 20 Barra Close, Highworth, Swindon, Wiltshire SN6 7HX
- **or scan and email** this form to info@stedwardspress.co.uk

Your details

Please send me ____ copies of BRUSSELS LAID BARE
(ISBN 978-0-9554188-1-5)

My name is _____

Please send the order to_____

_____

_____Post Code_____

Telephone _____

Email _____

Price: Single copies by post £12, including post and packing. For two or more copies apply a 20% discount.

Paying by cheque

I enclose a cheque for £ _____
(make cheques payable to St Edwards Press Ltd)

Paying by credit card

Card Number _____

Name on card _____

Type of card_____

Expiry date____/_____

Security number - i.e. last three digits on reverse of card _____

Signature _____

Date _____

Please allow 28 days for delivery